GROUP REPRESENTATION, FEMINIST THEORY, AND THE PROMISE OF JUSTICE

Election Law, Politics, and Theory

Series Editor: David Schultz

Election Law, Politics, and Theory broadly examines election law at the national, subnational, and international or comparative levels. Titles in the series provide both empirical and theoretical analysis of topics and issues that affect voting, campaigns, and elections, and as such offer coverage of political as well as legal concerns and controversies. Useful for scholars, researchers, and practitioners in the field, volumes address such subjects as voting rights, reapportionment, ballot access, campaign finance reform, the courts and election regulation, and the role of actors including political parties and the media. The series' ultimate goal is to build scholarship in this key area by seeking to understand how elections function in an increasingly complex, technological, and global community, and the ways in which election law impacts outcomes, disputes, and eventually governance in particular nations and societies.

Other titles in this series

Political Parties and Elections
Legislating for Representative Democracy
Anika Gauja
ISBN 978 0 7546 7704 8

Electoral College Reform
Challenges and Possibilities
Edited by Gary Bugh
ISBN 978 0 7546 7751 2

State Secretaries of State
Guardians of the Democratic Process
Jocelyn F. Benson
ISBN 978 0 7546 7745 1

The Battle Over Bilingual Ballots
Language Minorities and Political Access Under the Voting Rights Act
James Thomas Tucker
ISBN 978 0 7546 7572 3

Group Representation, Feminist Theory, and the Promise of Justice

ANGELA D. LEDFORD
The College of Saint Rose, USA

Routledge
Taylor & Francis Group
LONDON AND NEW YORK

First published 2012 by Ashgate Publishing

Published 2016 by Routledge
2 Park Square, Milton Park, Abingdon, Oxfordshire OX14 4RN
711 Third Avenue, New York, NY 10017, USA

First issued in paperback 2016

Routledge is an imprint of the Taylor & Francis Group, an informa business

British Library Cataloguing in Publication Data
Ledford, Angela D.
Group representation, feminist theory, and the promise of justice. -- (Election law, politics, and theory)
1. Social groups--Political aspects. 2. Social justice.
3. Politics and culture. 4. Political participation.
5. Equality before the law. 6. Representative government and representation. 7. Feminist theory.
I. Title II. Series
320'.011-dc23

Library of Congress Cataloging-in-Publication Data
Ledford, Angela D.
Group representation, feminist theory, and the promise of justice / by Angela D. Ledford.
p. cm. -- (Series Election law, politics, and theory)
Includes bibliographical references and index.
ISBN 978-1-4094-1843-6 (hardback) 1. Feminist theory. 2. Women--Legal status, laws, etc. 3. Feminist jurisprudence. 4. Equality before the law. 5. Sex discrimination against women--Law and legislation. I. Title.
K349.L43 2012
346.01'34--dc23

2012027617

ISBN 13: 978-1-138-27881-3 (pbk)
ISBN 13: 978-1-4094-1843-6 (hbk)

Group Representation, Feminist Theory, and the Promise of Justice

ANGELA D. LEDFORD
The College of Saint Rose, USA

Routledge
Taylor & Francis Group
LONDON AND NEW YORK

First published 2012 by Ashgate Publishing

Published 2016 by Routledge
2 Park Square, Milton Park, Abingdon, Oxfordshire OX14 4RN
711 Third Avenue, New York, NY 10017, USA

First issued in paperback 2016

Routledge is an imprint of the Taylor & Francis Group, an informa business

British Library Cataloguing in Publication Data
Ledford, Angela D.
Group representation, feminist theory, and the promise of justice. -- (Election law, politics, and theory)
1. Social groups--Political aspects. 2. Social justice.
3. Politics and culture. 4. Political participation.
5. Equality before the law. 6. Representative government and representation. 7. Feminist theory.
I. Title II. Series
320'.011-dc23

Library of Congress Cataloging-in-Publication Data
Ledford, Angela D.
Group representation, feminist theory, and the promise of justice / by Angela D. Ledford.
p. cm. -- (Series Election law, politics, and theory)
Includes bibliographical references and index.
ISBN 978-1-4094-1843-6 (hardback) 1. Feminist theory. 2. Women--Legal status, laws, etc. 3. Feminist jurisprudence. 4. Equality before the law. 5. Sex discrimination against women--Law and legislation. I. Title.
K349.L43 2012
346.01'34--dc23

2012027617

ISBN 13: 978-1-138-27881-3 (pbk)
ISBN 13: 978-1-4094-1843-6 (hbk)

Contents

Preface		*vii*
1	Political Participation, Electoral Reform, and Social Difference: A New Politics of Representation?	1
2	Lani Guinier: Feminist Jurisprudence and Fair Representation	21
3	Feminism and Democracy: Anne Phillips and the Politics of Equality	47
4	Iris Marion Young and the Politics of Difference	67
5	Representation and the Politics of Democratic Inclusion	89
6	Social Class, Political Representation, and Democratic Revival: Resisting Quiescence and Manufactured Interests	109
7	Conclusion: A Feminist Politics of Inclusion	129
Bibliography		*139*
Index		*151*

For Kieran, Cole, and Cora Belle

Preface

This project began a number of years ago when I was at the University of South Carolina. It was thus carefully nurtured by scholars who I am proud to now stand with as colleagues: Laura Woliver, Dan Sabia, Jill Frank and Lynn Weber. It also greatly benefited at that time from conversations with my fellow friends and graduate students, Jack Lechelt, Janine Davidson, Paula L'Ecuyer, Ashlie Lancaster, Chris Dolan, Steve Campbell, Mike Grossman and Hans Von Rautenfeld.

Most of the actual writing of this project, however, took place at the College of Saint Rose, where I accepted a position soon after defending my dissertation proposal. Many people remarked that it must have been very hard to complete the dissertation while teaching a full load of courses. It certainly was not easy, but I owe an enormous debt to the College and many friends and colleagues who read chapters, listened to ideas I was trying to work out, shared fine beer with me, and welcomed me into an intellectual space that remains vibrant and inspiring. I am deeply grateful to the College of Saint Rose for its support of my work, notably through the released time I enjoyed as a resident fellow with the Center for Race and Ethnicity Studies. Among all of the wonderful colleagues I have at the College, none has been more supportive, encouraging or challenging than Carl Swidorski. He has read this manuscript, I am sure, more times than he cares to remember, and we have had innumerable conversations about key aspects of the project—especially the notion of "manufactured interests" that appears in Chapter 6. Those conversations were enriched significantly by Lisa Kannenberg, who often reminded me of the importance of historical specificity and context. I am indebted to her for her intellect and steadfast friendship. I also want to thank Richard Wunderlich, Sean Farrell, Jane Ladouceur, Risa Faussette, Ryane Straus, Jenise DePinto and Keith Haynes for reading and commenting on portions of the manuscript I was attempting to address with more clarity. That clarity has surely been improved by the fine editors at Ashgate and the thoughtful feedback from the series editor, David Schultz.

Finally, my family is truly remarkable. They are generous, kind and wise, and I am so grateful for their support and love. I owe more than I can say to Jeff Allen, Juretta and Jim Gonzales and Gary and Debra Ledford.

Angela D. Ledford
May 2012
Albany, New York

Chapter 1

Political Participation, Electoral Reform, and Social Difference: A New Politics of Representation?

> Luckily, the land between the extremes of group representation (to the exclusion of individual will) and individual representation (to the exclusion of group considerations) is not necessarily barren. (Elaine Spitz, *Majority Rule*, 1984, p. 50)

We have heard the dramatic yet serious pronouncements that we have reached the "end of history," the "end of ideology," and, most recently and pointedly, the "end of identity politics." This last pronouncement in particular strikes me as both wrong and dangerous. How can politics driven by one's gender, race, ethnicity, class and sexuality be at its end when inequality along these very same dimensions remains and, in some cases, is even on the rise? How can we hope to alter this trajectory if we continue to discount the evidence of its existence?

While the absolute political and economic conditions of women and minorities in the United States have risen, there remain stark inequalities compared with white America. "The median white household earned 62 per cent more income and possessed 12 times more wealth than the median black household; nearly two-thirds of black households (61 per cent), and half of Hispanic households have no net worth, while only a quarter of white Americans are in this predicament" (APSA Task Force Report 2004, p. 653). Racial and economic segregation in the public schools continues to rise (Frankenberg, Lee, and Orfield 2002). Incarceration rates of African-Americans and Latinos are radically disproportionate to their numbers in society compared with white offenders (US Department of Justice Prison Statistics 2004), and the disenfranchisement of non-incarcerated felons in numerous states exacerbates this very serious inequality by denying significant numbers of racial and ethnic minorities a voice in the polity (Manza and Uggen 2004). We continue to see a significant rise in economic inequality not only between the richest and poorest Americans but also between those considered upper vs middle class (APSA Task Force Report 2004). Those on the losing side of the widening wealth gap are too often racial and ethnic minorities. The poor are also disproportionately female and minority (Blau and Kahn 1994). Furthermore, while public opinion regarding gays and lesbians has continued to liberalize since the 1970s, hate crimes against sexual minorities continues unabated and, of all social groups, gays and lesbians rank among the lowest according to "feeling thermometer" ratings over the past 25 years (Yang 1997).

The ability to pursue a dignified and meaningful life is predicated on access to resources such as a quality education, physical health and safety, adequate housing, good jobs, and a sufficient income—measures that signal membership in the polity and make possible the achievement of a good life. That women and racial, ethnic and sexual minorities in America are over-represented on the lowest ends of many or most of these measures and under-represented on the higher side raises the specter of structural inequality. One of the most potent ways to address structural inequality is through political participation and representative government. Yet women and minorities are severely politically under-represented, in terms of both presence and interests. It is therefore imperative that we find alternative means by which to empower those on the margins as a matter of decency and as a matter of justice.

Yet how we think about those at the margins remains highly problematic. In *Hopwood v. Texas* (1996), a federal appeals court ruled that the University of Texas Law School could no longer use race as an element in making admissions decisions. "Almost overnight, the admissions officers at Rice [University] stopped saying aloud the words 'black,' 'African-American,' 'Latino,' 'Hispanic,' or even 'minority' in their deliberations. The next year, the proportion of black students admitted in the freshman class fell by half; the proportion of Hispanics fell by nearly a third" (Steinberg 2002, p. 22). In an effort to sidestep the *Hopwood* directive and forestall decreasing minority enrollment, Rice University developed some innovative tactics. Rice University officials,

> with an undisguised wink, [have] encouraged applicants to discuss 'cultural traditions' in their essays, asked if they spoke English as a second language and taken note, albeit silently, of those identified as presidents of their black student associations. Those efforts, along with stepped-up recruiting at high schools with traditionally high minority populations, yielded a freshman class last year with a near-record composition of blacks and Hispanics. Of the 700 freshmen, 7 percent are black, 11 percent are Hispanic. (p. 45)

In the summer of 2003, the US Supreme Court heard two cases that promised to test the constitutionality of the use of race by institutions of higher education in admissions decisions (and potentially Affirmative Action more generally). The target for the first case was the use of race as a factor for admission to the undergraduate program at the University of Michigan, while the second questioned using race to help determine slots for admission to the University of Michigan's School of Law. Very generally, the majority opinion was that race could continue to be used as one factor among many in making admission decisions (this from the undergraduate case). However, race cannot play too much of a role (which the majority warned that the law school had come too close to doing). The court acknowledged that race is a social reality that must be taken into consideration when making decisions about the distribution of limited goods, but granting it too much importance runs the risk of setting unqualified students up for failure and, even more important for some members of the court, treads perilously close to advocating quotas and thus offending the value of merit and desert. While there was some, although very limited, recognition of the existence of structural inequality and the impact that it can have on individual achievement, there was more emphasis on the value of a diverse student population for all students. In addition, at least for Sandra Day O'Connor in the Michigan law school case, a serious importance must be placed on diversity in the ranks of law school students given that law degrees so often grant entrée into positions of power—one of the greatest being national elective office (since Congress disproportionately comprises attorneys). However, in February of 2012, the court agreed to hear a major case that challenges race-conscious admissions at the University of Texas. There can be little doubt that this move signals the court's eagerness to reassess the use of race as a factor in admission to institutions of higher education.

These recent court decisions underscore the divisiveness in America surrounding the meaning of social difference. Is it fair to consider an individual's race, class, gender or sexuality when deciding on the allocation of scarce goods or opportunities? Is it fair not to? If it is fair, then *how* should social difference be considered? What weight should it be accorded? A majority on the Supreme Court maintains that race is a legitimate factor for making admissions decisions, but it cannot be too much of a factor. So how much of a factor is too much, too little and just right—and who decides? If we maintain that the distribution of goods should be solely based on merit, then how shall we determine what is "meritorious" achievement; how shall we address what is sure to be an increase in the existing inequality between whites and non-whites, men and women, the economically privileged and the struggling; and who shall make these determinations?

While some members of the Supreme Court (and a majority of Americans) are optimistic that policies such as Affirmative Action are nearing (or should be nearing) the end of their usefulness, most social indicators belie any such expectation. To remain with the example of higher education, while SAT scores have risen to their highest average since 1974, there remain important and significant gaps between white students and non-Asian minorities such that "the white–black gap was 187 points 10 years ago, 206 points today; Mexican-Americans trailed whites by 127 points in 1993 and are now 158 points back" (Bérubé 2003, p. 18). In fact there is a strong correlation between scores and income: "a combined 864 for test takers from households making under $10,000, 1,123 for kids from households making $100,000 and up—a differential of 259 points over $90,000, just as if you were to award students an SAT point for every $350 their parents take home" (p. 18). Yet when these indicators are combined for a broader pictures, it is the racial disparity that is "the key statistic for policy makers and pundits, because it has such somber implications for affirmative action. If SAT scores continue to follow the pattern of the past 10 years, college admissions boards will have to keep finding substantive, defensible and creative ways of enhancing minority enrollment despite the test numbers. And they will be roundly criticized for doing so" (p. 18).

If these scores are any indication of the status and meaningfulness of social difference in the American context, then there is not much reason for optimism that the need for Affirmative Action and similar programs will decline. The necessity for Affirmative Action programs will certainly not diminish without recognition of the structural nature of the inequality that coincides in disproportionate numbers with the least powerful members of the polity—women and racial and ethnic minorities.

The Supreme Court's Michigan cases highlight the central focus of this project: if social difference cannot be ignored without serious deleterious consequences, but according it too much weight or too little is associated with possibly even more negative outcomes than not considering it at all, then the stakes are very high for arriving at any conclusion. At the same time, answering these complex questions regarding difference and disagreement is a matter of democratic judgment. That judgment cannot be truly democratic or just, however, unless all relevant members of the polity are fully included at all stages of deliberation and decision making.

However, there is a clear and observable lack of women, people of color, gays, lesbians, the working class and the poor in representative bodies. Under-representation exists when members of discernible groups are not consistently present in representative bodies and among measures of well-being in numbers roughly proportionate to their populations. These groups are discernible based on a history and ongoing legacy of disenfranchisement usually marked by gender, race, ethnicity, class, sexuality and religion. Under-representation on basic social and economic measures, such as adequate housing, income, education and physical health, generally coincides with a history of disregard, deprivation and even violence. Access to these basic social goods is necessary to pursue a dignified life and is a prerequisite for the enjoyment of the political liberties of democratic citizenship. When access to these goods concurs with markers of social and political marginalization or exclusion, the exercise of political rights and obligations and achievement of the good life, however defined, is severely compromised.

The dimensions of under-representation in any society coincide with the access to and exercise of power. Historically it has been the case that those with power use their influence to define full membership in the polity to include themselves and similar subjects while defining out those they designate as different. That difference is not without judgment, however, but instead defined as inferiority to the privileged groups and corrosive to the community. In some instances groups want to assert their social difference but seek to change how a community values it. This is often the case with ethnicity, where the group wishes to maintain its cultural ways of life but demands fair recognition and accommodation of their existence from the state and other members of the polity. However in other instances, members of disadvantaged social groups regard their "group" status as illegitimate altogether and strive to dismantle its very meaning and any associated punishments. The goal in this regard is elimination of the status of "group." Some consider gender to be an appropriate example of this perspective.

Fair political representation is essential since it is a key democratic activity geared toward generating legitimacy, setting agendas, and establishing practices and policies under which we live. When identifiable groups of citizens are not present in adequate numbers over time, it tends to be the case that their interests and concerns are also absent, and thus under-representation exists. That women and racial, ethnic, religious and sexual minorities are over-represented on the lowest ends of most measures of social and political well-being and under-represented on the higher side raises the specter of structural inequality. Structural inequality exists when measures of the good life and indicators of deprivation are visibly and measurably stratified along these lines.

At a minimum and most generally, "we show a government to be representative not by demonstrating its control over its subjects but just the reverse, by demonstrating that its subjects have control over what it does" (Pitkin 1967, 232). Yet as democratic theorists from quite diverse perspectives have pointed out, this is only a jumping off point (Barber 1984; Benhabib 2002; Dahl 1963,

1972, 1989; Gutmann and Thompson 1996; hooks 1990, 1992; Mansbridge 1983; Rawls 1993, 1971; Walzer 1983; Williams 1998). Such definitions beg the questions *who* or *what* is to be represented, and under *what conditions* representation can be understood as democratic—even just?

Feminist Theory

Questions about difference and disagreement have been of particular interest within feminist theory. Of course it is not always clear what it means to "do" political theory, much less feminist theory. In fact, there are a number of ways in which scholars have approached political theory—some of which can be thought of as complementary (or at least not categorically opposed) to one another, while others are directly oppositional. "There is no way to formulate the problems of political philosophy that is politically or theoretically neutral. The manner in which one formulates the problem is in large part a function of one's own political priorities and of the methodological commitments implicit in one's conception of human nature" (Jaggar 1983, 133). Thus the differences we observe between thinkers are distinct not only because of the answers they provide but, maybe more importantly, because of the questions they ask. The three feminist theorists examined in this study illustrate this.

While these are questions of a distinctly methodological bent, they are necessarily tied up with an overarching aim in this project: to provide yet further support for the now more widely accepted claim that feminist theory has something distinctive and indispensable to offer political thought and practice. I say "necessarily tied up" because what we come to regard as the proper scope of political inquiry is intimately connected to our prior commitments to and investments in particular understandings of the political world and the agents that comprise it. Feminist theory is not only a body of literature that forms a distinctive sub-field in political thought, it is also an approach or method that makes possible that body of literature. Feminist theory, like queer theory and postcolonial studies, expands the scope of politics; it leads to an explosion in inquiry regarding the exercise of power, the reach of the public sphere, the political relevance of the private, and the very subjects of politics.

So if our conceptions of the citizen have been fundamentally gendered and raced, as feminist theorists broadly contend, then all of the key concepts and practices that build upon them must be gendered and raced as well (also see Baer 1999; Benhabib 1992, 1996; Brown 1995; Butler and Scott 1992; Hirschmann and Di Stefano 1996; hooks 1990, 1992; MacKinnon 1989; Minow 1990, 1997; Nussbaum 1999; Okin 1999; Pateman 1988, 1989; Phillips 1991, 1993, 1995, 1999; and Young 1997, 2000, 1990: feminist scholars who are asking different questions and approaching them from rather diverse perspectives, yet who all are making the case, to one degree or another, that feminist theory does not simply mean adding gender, race and class to an existing body of thoughtbut instead is a way of viewing phenomena that questions the adequacy or legitimacy of that very body of thought). This means that the ways in which we have institutionalized citizenship, particularly representation, "fit" or "work for" those privileged by their race, gender, class, ethnicity and sexuality better than for those not so situated.

So instead of simply adding women and minorities to the existing citizenship mix and stirring, we must revisit who the citizen is and how reconceiving the citizen affects how we evaluate the inclusiveness of the polity and the mechanisms designed to insure the just distribution of goods. For Shane Phelan, revisiting the citizen means "getting specific" about the experiences of members of disadvantaged groups that seriously impinge upon these individuals' ability to effectively function while clothed in the garments of citizenship that were designed for others, yet purport to be "one size fits all." Thus

> [o]pening the space of citizenship addresses the needs of U.S. lesbians for recognition and self-determination, inclusion, and safety. It also provides a means of linking lesbian struggles to other demands for these same things without assuming a priority among those struggles or suggesting a hierarchy of oppressions. It enables lesbians and others to be specific about their own circumstances and those of others, and to formulate a common agenda for concrete changes that does not play into zero-sum games of power. The demand for the broadest range of civil rights is not a 'special interest' demand, sought at the expense of the civic good or that of another 'group,' but is a demand for equal membership in a democratic polity. (Phelan 1994, 113)

By problematizing the very notion of citizenship, Phelan, among other feminist scholars, has attempted to move the debate beyond claims of "special rights," that only serve to reinforce the presumed fairness of existing practices and institutions, to demands for inclusion and fair recognition in the polity.

Many feminist theorists are thus unsatisfied with and wary of theories of representation that fail to interrogate the possibility of gendered and raced assumptions and pay sufficient heed to the practical realities of systemic inequality. As a result of this dissatisfaction, a number of feminist theorists have turned to group representation as an alternative to the so-called representation of individuals, which they argue works even occasionally only for those already privileged by their race, class, gender, ethnicity and/or sexuality (Guinier 1994, 1995; hooks 1992; Phillips 1993, 1995, 1998, 1999; Squires 2000; Weber 2001; and Young 1993, 1997, 2000).

Design and Approach

The vast majority of contemporary feminist theorists agree that there should be equality *through* (rather than in spite of) difference. The form that "equality through difference" takes, however, varies on the basis of how particular scholars understand difference and the role it plays in the polity, which then has an effect on the types of policies advocated to attempt to remedy representational inequality. In this project, I will highlight the work of Lani Guinier, Anne Phillips and Iris Marion Young. I chose to concentrate on these three scholars for three reasons. First, these are the feminist scholars who deal most specifically and effectively with the issue of social difference and political representation. Second, partially because of the aforementioned, these are the most often cited feminist theorists when it comes to issues of difference and representation. Third, a careful analysis of these three scholars allows me to make a case for special representation rights for historically marginalized groups.

In the following chapters, I will elucidate (1) how three key feminist theorists conceive of group representation, (2) what the problems are that group representation claims to remedy (these are at least partially dependent upon the answers to the first question), and (3) the strengths and weaknesses associated with these conceptions. I conclude that any conception of fair representation (or the representation of interests) must draw on the insights of feminist jurisprudence, feminist democratic theory and feminist identity politics. It must do so in order to maximize votes counted, and foster a more robust understanding of equality through political participation and measures that re-evaluate and alter the connections between meaningful recognition as a citizen and social class. Any group representation plan must also interrogate the ways in which social difference informs agency, recognition and interests in order that new and emancipatory forms of political engagement are encouraged.

Lani Guinier

For Lani Guinier the US system of political representation, based upon single-member geographic districts, proves problematic in that it wastes votes while pitting potential allies against one another or separating actual allies from each other through the districting process (both of which tend to become more prominent in the cases of race-conscious districting). The severity of these problems would be ameliorated, according to Guinier, by adopting a system that employs cumulative voting within multi-member districts where significant numbers of citizens embrace the concept of political race. Cumulative voting and multi-member districts would go a long way toward remedying the problem of wasted votes.

When joined with a "politicized" conception of race that diagnoses systemic oppression while unearthing the linked fates of African Americans and poor whites, increased political participation driven by coalitions of racially and economically disadvantaged citizens can and should fill the gaps left in the wake of electoral reform. I argue that Guinier recognizes wasted votes as a central representational problem because her analysis is driven by an assumption that electoral reform is the primary venue for remedying many of our representational woes; and what electoral reform cannot accomplish must be addressed *external* to the formal political sphere by locating some basis upon which disadvantaged citizen groups can recognize the similarities of their structured existences.

This recognition can and should, on Guinier and Gerald Torres's account, encourage a more robust and effective form of coalition-based political participation that will render electoral reform meaningful by producing candidates and policies that reflect the interests of previously inert citizen groups. While I find the electoral reform that Guinier offers quite attractive, the concept of political race that should put such reforms to work through heightened participation (1) is ultimately too narrow to accomplish the task, and (2) mistakenly places the initial emphasis for increased participation on the recognition by members of racially and economically disadvantaged groups of their linked condition rather than the provision of economic resources that would lower the burdens of *initiating* collective action.

Guinier provides a basis for much-needed electoral reform that bodes well for the improvement of the representation of relevant interests. However she is loath to single out groups for special consideration. She and Torres develop a concept of political race that promises to diagnose instances of systemic inequality and unsheathe the cycles of economic dependency and disadvantage that masquerade as the outcomes of free choice and equal opportunity rather than institutional preferences. In accomplishing both of these tasks, political race connects a notion we are relatively more comfortable talking about (race) to get at something Americans are less comfortable confronting (class).

Political race then ought to demonstrate the linked condition of race and class—a link that should form the basis or justification for a political coalition of the racially and ethnically disadvantaged with the racially privileged but economically deprived. The concept of political race of Guinier and Torres, however, is not broad enough to encompass all relevant social differences, particularly when it comes to gender and sexuality, which will be elaborated in Chapter 2. Even if it was broad enough, it is not likely that the construct would encourage the participation necessary to energize historically disadvantaged groups and maintain that energy over time (thus effecting policy change). Empirical studies have indicated time and again that the important item that disadvantaged groups (with under-represented interests) lack that other groups do not *from the outset* is access to resources. Political race as a concept for diagnosing injustice and encouraging coalitions may well be useful once groups have mobilized, but it is not enough to initiate that mobilization. Guinier seeks to answer the question, "How can electoral reform be meaningful?"

Anne Phillips

Where Guinier seems to neglect gender when it comes to the notion of political race, Anne Phillips does almost the opposite by using gender as her centerpiece (along with class), while neglecting race and ethnicity. Phillips, like Guinier (although in a much more sustained fashion than the latter) rejects a robust conception of group representation because of its tendency to freeze differences. By "freezing differences" she means that the very act of categorizing a group of citizens based particularly on aspects of their identity (their race, ethnicity, religion or sexuality, for example) is premised on an assumption or set of assumptions about the shared characteristics of the members of that group that justify placing them in a group at all. The danger of such an activity comes about when citizens are grouped under group monikers that have little or no meaning for how they live their lives, or when the characteristics that are thought to be shared by a group are in fact sharply contested.

Phillips also rejects a robust form of group representation because, even if there was a way to avoid fixing interests in the process of creating and recognizing groups based on social difference, the question remains which groups to recognize as deserving scrutiny and who would decide. Instead Phillips proposes gender quotas at the party list stage (and advances a proposal for gender convergence to displace the sexual division of labor and possibly even the mal-distribution of wealth in general). Phillips calls for gender quotas (while specifically rejecting "group representation"), racial and ethnic "targets," and a norm of convergence because she fails to take seriously the ways in which social difference truly matters for structuring and conditioning interests. Ironically, both Guinier and Phillips write fairly extensively on the importance of class and the ways in which it structures political inequality, yet neither endorses the kind of public financing that would equalize access to the resources essential to get mobilization off the ground. However both Guinier and Phillips are in agreement that marking off "groups" in any formal sense poses the familiar (and in their estimation irresolvable) problems of which groups count, who decides, and how can the recognition of groups avoid the stigmatizing effects of assuming some set of shared interests? Hence Phillips asks, "What does equality allow?"

Iris Marion Young

Iris Marion Young provides potential answers to these questions about conditions under which groups might be cordoned off from one another. She argues for the representation of structural groups, the members of which will often not share the same interests, but will nevertheless often share a social perspective based on similar experiences of difference—something that can and should be represented within a more deliberative and participatory public sphere.

For Young, race, gender, ethnicity and sexuality are best understood as "structures" rather than some set of ascriptive characteristics. A focus on ascriptive characteristics leads to a dangerous essentialism that naturalizes differences, makes inequality impervious to change, and does little to identify shared concerns or generate effective mobilization. Instead, race, gender, ethnicity and sexuality are systems of power that exclude and diminish. If we understand social difference in this way, according to Young, the evidence of marginalization and repression reveals itself along structural lines. Measures of the good life will be disproportionately led by the privileged, while women and minorities will be over-represented among people living lives of deprivation. These measures of existence structure the lives of those who live within their confines. Such experiences, Young explains, comprise a roughly shared group outlook or perspective. It is not particularly coherent to argue that women and minorities share some set of interests. However because one's experiences tend to be structured in particular ways when one is a member of a disadvantaged group, Young argues that a shared outlook is often the result. That shared perspective is the foundation for mobilization and group representation rights.

However, ultimately Young goes too far by not heeding Phillips's well-placed concerns about further stigmatizing and straitjacketing groups. Young does not taking seriously enough the fluid and cross-cutting nature of group membership (and in fact the very meaning of group membership). Young inquires, "How can the inclusion of social difference be required?"

Inclusive Representation: A Feminist Intersectional Standpoint

I conclude that the feminist theories of Guinier, Phillips and Young provide particular and necessary resources for answering representational questions, but that each of these offerings is partial in its own way. Only by taking particular contributions of each do we get a compelling theory of how real inclusion through difference might look.

Guinier's electoral reform goes a good way toward rectifying the worth of the ballot, but her work fails to provide the necessary conditions for initiating the political participation beyond voting that is the necessary corollary of fair and effective representation. Wary of according too much meaning to marginalized groups by singling them out for special consideration, Phillips rejects "group representation" in favor of party list quotas and racial and ethnic targets. Yet Phillips actually endorses a weak form of group representation while refusing to recognize the ways in which identity has meaning based not on biological characteristics but rather the exercise of power that presses women and minorities to the margins.

Young's scholarship identifies the structural nature of social difference that answers much of Phillips's strong yet wise objections. Young's contribution allows her to make the case for determining which groups get to count as groups worthy of scrutiny. However making this determination is both her greatest and her most problematic achievement. On the one hand, we now have a basis for determining which groups count for the distribution of public resources for political organization and mobilization. These resources are a necessary element for *initiating* participation, but both Guinier and Phillips reject them because of their unease with the degree to which members of historically disadvantaged groups share interests. This unease, I maintain, is not without merit as Young invests too much weight in the meaning of these social differences so that the group representation she ultimately endorses indeed falls prey to the very kinds of problems that Phillips, in particular, lays out. I maintain that a careful balance can be struck on the issue of group representation, one that takes seriously the differences that make a difference while eluding the straight-jacketing of identity and legitimizing the power dynamics that provide their meaning.

In order for fair representation, (1) citizens' interests must be reflected by candidates of their choosing in meaningful public policies and practices, (2) their social perspectives or ways of life should be valued and protected by a form of group representation that echoes the lived experiences of race, class, ethnicity, gender, sexuality and ability, and (3) their agency and accountability should be encouraged while limiting essentialism and stagnation.

Deborah Stone writes that "[r]epresentation is the process by which interests are defined and activated in politics" (Stone 2002, 215). Stone goes on to point out that representation has a "dual quality."

> [R]epresentatives give expression to an interest by portraying an issue, showing how it affects people and persuading them that the portrait is accurate; and representatives speak for people in the sense of standing for them and articulating their wishes in policy debates. The paradox is that what representatives say when they speak for their constituents is not the constituents' own words (figuratively speaking), but words the representatives composed and used to persuade their constituents in the first place. (Stone 2002, 215)

This paradox is different than the one identified by Hannah Pitkin. For Pitkin, "true political representation requires that a representative must do what his or her constituents want, but on the other hand, it requires that the representative do what he or she thinks best" (Stone 2002, 215). However, Stone is careful to remark that this "balance" might not do the trick—particularly when there exist structural divisions that inform the mal-distribution of power. Stone explains,

> Rather, when one or two demographic characteristics, such as race, religion, or gender, are important determinants of power and opportunity in a society, then those characteristics must form the basis of representation in order to ensure that people on the weak side of the dividing line are represented. In a society where race is an important political dividing line and a factor that deeply shapes people's political views, minorities may need representatives of their own race. Where gender is an important determinant of political power and policy attitudes, men may not adequately represent women. (Stone 2002, 359–60)

Political representation is a crucial site of analysis since it is a key democratic activity geared toward setting agendas and establishing practices and policies under which we live. It is therefore imperative that all relevant members of the polity have a real say in all stages of this process. When identifiable groups of citizens are not present (and their interests are perpetually ignored or defeated), we must seek other measures that will make inclusion a reality.

Groups and Interests

Ultimately I argue that disadvantaged structural groups should be provided with federally funded resources to self-organize and advocate slates of candidates that share their interests within large multi-member jurisdictions that employ a system of semi-proportional representation through cumulative voting. Taking into account social difference when devising electoral arrangements that seek to deliver fair representation is necessary to satisfy the requirements of justice. In doing so, we need not make any *a priori* assumptions or draw any conclusions about the content of shared interests, concerns or perspectives that are necessarily affixed to race or gender, for example, any more than we make claims about the essential nature of those who identify with the Democratic or Republican party. The partisan "moniker" is a proxy for interests that develop and shift based on experiences—experiences that are fundamentally (although certainly not solely) conditioned and structured by race, class, ethnicity, gender and sexuality.

The representation of interests is the best way to recognize particularity. The emphasis on interests reflects attention to the ways in which preferences and concerns can cut across traditional identity lines, while careful highlighting of groups indicates a refusal to ignore the meaning collective identifications hold for life chances and self-understandings, all of which condition citizen interests. I thus use *interests* not in the Burkean sense of a "trustee" relationship in which the representative is to reflect the "enlightened" (and thus fairly fixed) interests of the nation rather than the mere self-interested "preferences" of the individual or district. Instead I regard interests here much in the same way as Jane Mansbridge does in a recent piece on the normative implications of key forms of representation in empirical political science. She writes,

> [i]n this analysis the preferences and interests into which deliberation should provide insight may be self-regarding, other-regarding, or ideal-regarding. I thus use the word 'interest' in its American, rather than European, sense to include foundational (that is, identity-constituting) ideal-regarding commitments as well as material needs and wants. Because transforming identities transforms interests, interests can be seen as both 'enlightened preferences' (with 'enlightenment' seen as the product of experiences and emotional understanding as well as of simple cognition) and as changeable and contested. (Mansbridge 2003, 517)

What I particularly like about Mansbridge's conception of interests is the way she regards them as fundamentally and importantly related to experiences that are structured and conditioned by one's identity. Identity, it is important to point out, does not simply mean how we think about or define ourselves but more importantly the ways in which we are recognized or perceived by others based on possession of characteristics that have societal meaning for the purposes of the distribution, maintenance and justification of power.

While we can certainly say that individuals have interests, it is often the case that those interests arise as the result of experiences. No experiences are more important with regards to one's life chances than those structured by the systemic exercise of power, which is the necessary foundation of the social meanings of racial, class, ethnic, gender and sexual differences. Myriad occurrences can affect one's interests. Yet the experiences of race, class, ethnic, gender and sexual difference in the American context cannot help but influence one's outlook given that we have assigned such prominence to these differences.

Thus interests tend to have a group characteristic. This hardly means that all members of some racial group will share the same interests. Rather it means that we should not be surprised that more blacks than whites favor Affirmative Action or that the working class and poor tend to support increased federal spending for social services. Being a member of a disadvantaged race or class clearly figures prominently in arriving at some set of interests. This is especially so since one's lifetime experiences have been structured in important ways by the possession of one or more of these group characteristics. This does not mean, however, that possession of one or more of these markers will structure one's interests in any singular direction. Kristin Luker, in her seminal work on abortion, makes a similar point when she explains how women became abortion activists on opposing sides of the debate.

> In short, in a world where men and women have traditionally had different roles to play and where male roles have traditionally been the more socially prestigious and financially rewarded, abortion has become a symbolic marker between those who wish to maintain this division of labor and those who wish to challenge it. Thus, on an intimate level, the pro-life movement is women's version of what was true of peasants in the Vendée, the part of France that remained Royalist during the French Revolution. Charles Tilly has argued that in the Vendée, traditional relationships between nobles and peasants were still mutually satisfying so that the 'brave new world' of the French Revolution represented more loss than gain, and the peasants therefore resisted the changes the Revolution heralded. By the same logic, traditional relationships between men and women are still satisfying, rewarding, and meaningful for pro-life women, and they therefore resist the lure of 'liberation.' For pro-choice women, however, with their access to male resources, a division of labor into the public world of work and the private world of home and hearth seems to promise only restriction to 'second-class' citizenship. (Luker 1984, 201–202)

Luker unambiguously asserts that gender is one of the central prisms though which women perceive the abortion issue. Nevertheless, it is one's *experience* of gender, conditioned by other contributory factors such as access to, familiarity with, and success in the public sphere, that is crucial for understanding different attitudes within a category.

Luker goes on to write that the life circumstances of pro-choice and pro-life women offer important insight into why natural family planning is popular among pro-life supporters but almost wholly rejected by pro-choice people.

> The pro-choice women we met have approximately the same kinds of education as their husbands do, and many of them have the same kinds of jobs—they are lawyers, physicians, college professors, and the like. Even those who do not work in traditionally male occupations have jobs in the paid labor market and thus share common experiences. They and they husbands share many social resources in common: they both have some status outside the home, they both have a paycheck, and they both have a set of peers and friends located in the work world rather than in the family world. In terms of the traditional studies of family power, pro-choice husbands and wives use the same bargaining chips and have roughly equal amounts of them. (Luker 1984, 213)

Access to social and economic power is an important factor in explaining divergent positions on abortion among women. It would be a mistake, however, to read Luker as discounting gender altogether. Gender recedes as an explanatory element only when power relations are roughly equal. That is rarely the case when judged from the macro-level. Thus gender does not determine a person's abortion attitudes. Yet it does, in a context of unequal power, condition one's attitude in important ways.

The serious power disparity that Luker identifies is also important for the ways in which it contributes to the emergence of activism. In fact the existence of such social cleavages has led and continues to lead to extra-institutional mass mobilization—a phenomenon that pluralists, for example, have been hard-pressed to explain in light of what they claim to be fairly formal institutional and jurisprudential equality. Why would disaffected individuals take the time and effort and even risk grave danger to band together to press their claims in the streets and hallways of governments when there are available institutional mechanisms enforced by an impartial and responsive state?

Social movement and contentious politics scholars have approached this question from a variety of perspectives. Resource mobilization and rational choice scholars such as Mancur Olson (1965) take a decidedly individualist approach and argue that individuals are most likely to participate in groups when there exist individual material rewards for doing so. While Olsen acknowledged that there are sometimes non-material incentives for collective behavior, such as solidary and purposive benefits, those motivations are generally secondary to, or at the very least must be combined with, material rewards. Another group of scholars claim that individuals rebel as the result of relative deprivation, when a threshold in the gap between what one has and what one expects is felt (Gurr 1971). Still others maintained that contentious behavior comes about with the rise of the nation state (Tilly 1984, 1990), increased access to resources and political opportunities (Costain 1992), and as part of historical cycles of protest (McAdam 1982; Tarrow 1998).

The existence of these movements has not, however, led to widespread recognition that the United States possesses serious social cleavages. The reasons for why we have been so hesitant about, and even hostile to, providing institutional remedies for social inequality are varied and complex. However, two recent occurrences led me to a very basic conclusion: as a nation, we simply do not regard our social differences as comparable in depth and meaning to those we observe beyond our borders.

The early works on political development by Arend Lijphart, Gabriel Almond, Talcott Parsons, Lucian Pye and G. Bingham Powell Jr include stunning comparisons and typologies that mostly considere American political culture (and much of Anglo-Western political culture) to be homogenous, sharing a commitment to the same set of political and social values when measured against much of the non-Anglo Western world. While some of these specific comparisons hold up better than others, and all of these scholars have subsequently refined their scholarship, what occurred to me when reading this material again after something like 12 years was the very deep assumption that, although differences exist in the United States, they are far from deep cleavages along which citizens forge discernible interests and ways of life. If anything, these differences were viewed as minor in duration given their very thin existence just atop an overriding and thoroughgoing commitment to "American values" as well as an assumption of systemic, institutional fairness. Those places with *truly* deep cleavages, political development scholars at the time tended to claim, were either doomed to authoritarian rule or, on the more optimistic side, might successfully pursue a power-sharing system of governance (consociational democracy). At no point, at least at this stage in the literature, was there much consideration of the possibility that social difference in the American context might be significant enough to warrant the application of similar remedies. It is an American exceptionalism of the worst sort that denies a history of violence and disagreement not completely dissimilar to countries for which scholars deemed consociationalism or other such inclusive governance appropriate.

The second event occurred not long after reviewing this American political development scholarship. As the Bush Administration continued in its unilateralist foreign policy in Iraq, I was surprised to hear Administration spokespersons speak forcefully and clearly on the need for proportional representation and some form of power-sharing along the various religious and ethnic cleavages in order for the new Iraqi government to be truly legitimate—this from an administration that only acknowledges the ethos of individualism and a singular governing majority. We do not hear such proposals mentioned as potential remedies for American inequalities. Advocating such measures would be an admission of the existence of cleavages and systemic inequalities that would undermine our national identity. Hence the stakes are high for maintaining the veneer of equality of opportunity, systemic impartiality and justice through plurality rule.

Group representation is justified because failure to do so violates the principle of inclusion, disregards the principle of equality, and encourages and reinforces injustice (or systemic biases). It is my intention to encourage more vibrant political participation by members of marginalized groups in order to facilitate more effective and fair representation. Electoral reform, while important, is not enough. There need to be meaningful incentives for citizens to do things differently, which means that we must secure measures to increase political resources and influence over policy by disadvantaged groups (throughout this project I refer to "disadvantaged," "historically marginalized," and "structural" groups, all of which are used interchangeably).

A careful analysis of the scholarship of Guinier, Phillips and Young provides the opportunity to make a solid case for both serious electoral reform (which is neutral on social difference) *and* for the provision of public funds for marginalized groups (which is animated by and specifically directed toward eliminating inequitable treatment based on social difference). An examination of Guinier's work allows me to make a case for why race-neutral institutional change, even if coupled with extra-institutional difference-specific forms of political participation, is necessary but not sufficient to secure fair representation for historically marginalized groups.

When confronting whether formal, institutional recognition of difference is even possible and coherent, much less advisable, grappling with the work of Anne Phillips helps advance the argument. Through methodical analysis of her rejection of "group representation," I attempt to make a convincing case for its adoption. If the normative case for group representation is convincing, I have yet to establish its coherence and plausibility, especially with regard to the all-important question of how to determine which groups will count for special recognition.

In response to this question, Iris Young's work helps make a strong case for demonstrating how social difference is meaningful. Her understanding of social perspective possesses a coherence that should be articulated in representative fora. Fair and effective representation means that the least advantaged groups in a polity are both active and successful in nominating and electing slates of candidates that share group members' perspectives and outlooks. It also requires that these representatives be elected in sufficient numbers with good reasons and inducements to form coalitions with other marginalized groups to expand agendas, propose legislation, and craft and implement policies favorable to those disadvantaged communities.

All of this means that electoral reform is clearly required and desperately needed, for the current American system works well for so few. However, not just any electoral reform will do. While it is necessary to devise and implement electoral reform across the board for all citizens, justice requires specific measures that target those groups that have historically fallen on the wrong side of society's structures of power. These targets address systemic inequalities that difference-blind approaches cannot eliminate.

My argument charts a careful path along the razor's edge. It is an attempt to recognize the meaning and worth of social difference while rejecting the chains that so often bind difference to essence. In advocating both electoral change as well as providing federal funding for grassroots organization and mobilization, it is my intention to provide incentives for the increased participation of historically disadvantaged groups that will probably increase the numbers of members of such groups in elective bodies and expand the numbers and types of interests represented.

Chapter 2

Lani Guinier: Feminist Jurisprudence and Fair Representation

> The government of the American republics seems to me as centralized and more energetic than the absolute monarchies of Europe. So I do not think it will collapse from weakness. If ever freedom is lost in America, that will be due to the omnipotence of the majority driving the minorities to desperation and forcing them to appeal to physical force. We may then see anarchy, but it will have to come as the result of despotism. (de Tocqueville 1969, 260)

> And there is quite a lot of juice to be extracted from plumy reminiscences of 'individualism' and 'freedom' if the tree upon which such fruit hangs is a black population forced to serve as freedom's polar opposite: individualism is foregrounded (and believed in) when its background is stereotypified, enforced dependency. Freedom (to move, to earn, to learn, to be allied with a powerful centre, to narrate the world) can be relished more deeply in a cheek-by-jowl existence with the bound and unfree, the economically oppressed, the marginalized, the silenced. (Morrison 1997, 37)

Feminist legal theorists are in a particular predicament. Much of early feminist thought about the law (especially that hailing from critical legal theory) was situated, in important ways, around establishing that American jurisprudence is a highly subjective project, rather than the set of universal norms and standards it is so often presumed to be (see, for example, Ackerman 1984; Dworkin 1977, 2000; Raz 1983, 1994; Sunstein 1994). This early work pointed to the ways in which a legal system premised upon a gendered (i.e. male) conception of the citizen, but widely considered universal, in practice leads to unequal treatment.

Pregnancy (and the private sphere more generally) has been one of the key examples used to illustrate the law's gendered character. It is only when women begin to enter the public sphere in greater numbers that questions about maternity leave, pay and promotion begin to arise. The rise of these issues, and indeed their continued relevance, shows in stark relief the masculine character of the "worker." However, the law can also be a tool of resistance and empowerment. It can legitimize and make real the claims of the marginalized for inclusion and fairness in ways that other institutions and practices might not. If the law is an enunciation of our collective commitments at any given moment, then legal recognition is like an official imprimatur of belonging. So the predicament for feminist legal theorists is how to navigate the treacherous terrain between understanding the law as a historical artifact that did not have women in mind as the subjects of public life and regarding the law as an important site for securing rights and widespread recognition.

Legal Subjectivity?

There is a rich body of feminist scholarship that addresses the subjectivity of American law. The law is subjective insofar as it is based upon particular social experiences, in particular white, male, heterosexual, middle- to upper-class experiences. Nevertheless, there has been significant success in purging from American jurisprudence overtly discriminatory statutes. Yet the body of law that remains, while apparently "formally" equal, remains "substantively" less so.

> Given the occupational inequalities that remain, however, it is equally critical to understand the limitations of conventional legal strategies. Although they have been highly significant in challenging the most overt forms of gender discrimination, traditional equal-opportunity frameworks have not confronted the deeper institutional and ideological forces that contribute to gender disadvantage. (Rhode 1989, 176)

Those forces emerge from the sexual division of labor, in which women are disproportionately responsible for the activities broadly associated with the private sphere: child-rearing, household chores, sexual services and nurturing. Judith Baer writes that "the roots of law's maleness lie in men's division of life into public and private, justice and care, subject and object, rights and responsibility; and in men's assignment of women to specific spheres and duties" (Baer 1999, 70). For Martha Minow, "[o]nly by admitting our partiality can we strive for impartiality. Impartiality is the guise partiality takes to seal bias against exposure ... The idea of impartiality implies human access to a view beyond human experience, a 'God's eye' point of view. Not only do humans lack this inhuman perspective, but humans who claim it are untruthful, trying to exercise power to cut off conversation and debate" (Minow 1993, 313; see also Cornell 1992, 1999, 2000; Fineman 1991; Minow 1990, 1991). Furthermore,

> Legal decisions engrave upon our culture the stories we tell to and about ourselves, the meanings that constitute the traditions we invent. Searching for words to describe realities too multiple and complex to be contained by their language, litigants and judges struggle over what will be revealed and what will be concealed in the inevitable partiality of human judgment. Through

> deliberate attention to our own partiality, we can begin to acknowledge the dangers of pretended impartiality. (Minow 1993, 315)

It is important to bear in mind, however, that early legal challenges hinging on issues of equal and fair citizenship were lodged by relatively privileged white females. Stemming from the critical legal theory scholarship, critical race theory quickly followed to illustrate how the law was not only gendered but raced as well (Bell 1995, 2000; Crenshaw 1995, Dalton 1995; Guinier 1994; Harris 1995; Matsuda 1995, 1005; Roberts 1998; Williams 1992). Further challenges then ensued in the form of disabilities.

If the law is subjective in the ways these scholars pointed out, then how can we go about rectifying its unjust and unequal outcomes? Can we work through a system designed to privilege a class of citizens to which we do not belong? If we do, can we hope only for piecemeal reform and limited, albeit improved, citizenship? While recognizing that the law is both gendered and raced, feminist jurisprudence is nevertheless committed to mining the structures and practices of American law in an effort to craft more just political procedures and institutions. In placing the law at the center of their analyses, feminist legal theorists ask in what ways do the law and legal practice inhibit the representation of the historically marginalized, and what resources does it provide for establishing better inclusiveness?

For Lani Guinier, fair representation can only exist when all relevant interests are included and possess the requisite force to affect outcomes. However our electoral system, comprising the laws, norms and practices that ought to institutionalize or approximate "representativeness," fails in key respects. In order to achieve something like fair representation, Guinier argues, much as I will in the following chapters, that we must provide incentives for citizens to do things differently, which will require both electoral reform and some set of motivating factors to increase political engagement on the part of those at the margins.

Although electoral reform is important for Guinier and is likely to increase political participation somewhat, the increased participation necessary by members of disadvantaged groups cannot be expected from changes to electoral politics alone. Joining forces with Gerald Torres, Guinier develops a politicized conception of race that helps diagnose systemic inequality on the one hand, but also reveals how racial injustice and economic inequality (experienced by both people of color and whites) are linked and actually reinforce one another, a powerful foundation for justifying and encouraging increased and coalition-based civic engagement by the historically disadvantaged. The initial diagnosis of injustice (based on race) is the miner's canary that signals danger for everyone in the toxic environment. Looking closer, what seemed to be racial oppression is also connected to and reinforced by other systemic inequalities, particularly those revealed by class divisions. Racial oppression indicates deeper trouble because of both the unique history of race in America and a thoroughgoing unease in the United States with talking about and addressing social class.

As will become clear, I find the electoral reform proposed by Guinier extremely compelling and convincing. Her emphasis on increased political participation is key for rendering political representation meaningful. However I find the concept of political race to be lacking. First, political race lacks inclusivity by slighting important differences that can actually undermine the very coalitions Guinier and Torres seek to encourage. Second, political race, while effectively diagnosing systemic inequality and possibly serving to encourage cooperation across certain social differences, falls short of the mark for *initiating* political participation. However, before turning to the concept of political race, let us first address more systematically Guinier's analysis of the performance of American electoral practices and institutions and the changes she proposes to rectify their shortcomings.

Wasted Votes, Limited Choices and Bad Proxies

Guinier (1994) contends that the American electoral system is sorely inadequate in part because it wastes votes. Votes are wasted primarily because of single-member district, winner-takes-all elections based upon geographic districting. A winner-takes-all electoral system creates the well-known problem of awarding office to the candidate with only a plurality of the votes, leaving the remaining candidates and their voters with, presumably, nothing. This outcome might not be so problematic were it not for cyclical and permanent minorities, understood as those habitually left unrepresented (or under-represented) owing to their inability to elect a candidate of their choosing. These minorities are most often, as Guinier rightly points out, members of historically marginalized racial, ethnic and language groups. All those votes cast for the loser are, in effect, wasted votes (and not much faith can be placed in the idea that representation of even many interests is taking place). In fact, the votes cast for the winner in excess of what was necessary to elect her are also wasted votes "because they were unnecessary to provide an electoral margin within the district *and* they could have been used to provide the necessary electoral margin for a like-minded partisan in another district. In other words, packing voters in homogenous districts wasted votes because it dilutes their overall voting strength jurisdiction-wide" (Guinier 1994, 134).

This problem of "wasted votes" is particularly striking and strongest when there are many "safe seats," where the incumbent is unlikely to be defeated (Crigler, Just, and McCaffery 2004, 138). This situation increasingly characterizes the American electoral system, particularly given the rise of partisan gerrymandering evident in states such as Texas and Pennsylvania. In fact, "[o]nly four challengers defeated incumbents in the 2002 general elections, a record low, and in the nation's 435 Congressional districts, there may be no more than 30 this year where the outcome is truly in doubt" ("Fixing Democracy" 2004, 10).

Furthermore, "virtual representation" cannot fill in the gaps. Virtual representation is said to occur when the interests of those who cast votes for the loser in their district are represented by a like-minded representative in another district, are represented indirectly by the winner in the district in which they reside or are represented by virtue of the assumption that "the district itself is a cognizable group that is represented ultimately as a community of the whole" (Guinier 1995, 211). Yet this form of representation relies on a top-down view that dilutes and, in some cases, obliterates what citizens actually have to say. In fact, a reliance on virtual representation as a kind of "second best" fall-back position to ensure an adequate voice in the legislature almost completely ignores accountability, a key component of democratic representation. For how would a voter in District A hold a "virtual" representative in District B accountable without a vote to trade for possible re-election? The only way to maintain some form of accountability in such a scenario would be by the voter in District A giving or withholding campaign contributions (in lieu of the vote) to the preferred representative in District B. Jane Mansbridge discusses this relationship, which she refers to as "surrogate representation." She points out that "[b]ecause all the power that is exercised in any surrogate representation works through monetary or other contributions and through contributors rather than voters, surrogate representation in the United States today embodies far more political inequality than does even the traditional legislator-constituent relation" (Mansbridge 2003, 523).

Moreover, the problem is not simply one of race-conscious districting in particular, as many critics maintain, but rather one of districting in general.

> Winner-take-all territorial districting imperfectly distributes representation based on group attributes and disproportionately rewards those who win the representational lottery. Territorial districting uses an aggregating rule that inevitably groups people by virtue of some set of externally observed characteristics such as geographic proximity or racial identity. In addition, the winner-take-all principle inevitably wastes some votes. The dominant group within the district gets all the power; the votes of supporters of

> nondominant groups or of disaffected voters within the dominant group are wasted. Their votes lose significance because they are consistently cast for political losers. (Guinier 1994, 121)

Democracy requires that we extend to all citizens the "*equal opportunity to vote for a winning candidate* as a universal principle of political fairness" (Guinier 1994, 122), and this principle should apply to all voters. While racial group representation is important, Guinier points out, it is problematic for a couple of related reasons. On the one hand, the representation of groups is insufficiently realized under an electoral system based upon geographic districting. On the other, race, just like geography, is a poor proxy for interests—what we are and should be representing—given that not all members of a particular group will share the same interests, and "descriptive" representation, as Pitkin demonstrates, tells us very little about what a representative actually does and on whose behalf.

What is required is what Guinier calls "one vote, one value" or "proportional interest representation" based on cumulative voting. The intention here is to equalize the power or weight of the vote, something rendered virtually impossible under a system of territorial districting for the reasons stated above, so that citizens are more likely to have an equal opportunity to influence public policy. This opportunity to influence policy, Guinier argues, is what voting is all about, and if policy influence is dependent upon groups of citizens making their interests known, then a system of geographic districting that cordons off voters based upon where they reside also has the effect of isolating citizens from real or potential allies in other districts, ultimately diluting their potential for effecting policy change.

The move toward race-conscious districting beginning in the early 1960s was a logical, although flawed, means to correct poor representation. This limited representation was clearly evidenced, the courts maintained, by the paucity of black representatives in elective office. The assumption again was that voting is primarily about winning elections, and that more African-Americans in elective office would translate into better representation. Racial gerrymandering was the outcome. Congress drew a few majority minority districts, increasing the total number of minority representatives but not in sufficient numbers to regularly exercise power in decision-making. Furthermore, the drawing of majority minority districts had the effect of shoring up vast white electoral majorities with minorities essentially "packed" into a few isolated districts where their overall impact was diluted (Lublin 1999).

Not only is there an assumed direct connection between voting and winning elections, but the move toward racial gerrymandering revealed yet again the larger assumption about what we are representing and thus how representation should be translated into electoral practice. The one-person, one-vote rule has predominantly been a reflection of the individual right to participate in political life, at least on the American constitutional interpretation. However the idea behind that rule is based on the equal opportunity to have one's interests represented, a criterion that cannot be met under a system of geographic districting for all those reasons highlighted above. The fact that representation in the United States is based upon territorial districts, and that drawing districts along racial lines was for some time a legal practice, underscores the assumptions made about shared or group interests. Territorial districting is thought to protect communities of interest just like race-conscious districting.

While there are good reasons to suppose that voters in a geographic domain might very well share certain interests, there is much about which they will naturally disagree. Citizens often cannot pick up and move to a more agreeable district for obvious financial reasons, and it would be irrational for them to do so given that district lines will continue to be redrawn. Moreover, Guinier points out that citizens do not move to "districts." They move to or reside in neighborhoods—neighborhoods that are often not freely chosen but are open to citizens because of their race, ethnicity, and/or income. "Like family, geographic districts may not reflect conscious choice; as 'compulsory constituencies,' they nevertheless reflect ties that bind" (Guinier 1994, 129).

One of the key insights from Guinier then, at least for my purposes, is that districting in the United States reflects certain assumptions about interests, the key assumption being that interests are a group concept. Only by assuming that geography entails some set of shared and identifiable interests is the organization of voting along territorial lines coherent. While citizens who reside within a particular geographic region will certainly share some interests, such as price supports for territorially specific agricultural crops, geography will often not be the only or even the most relevant factor for ascertaining those interests. Reliance on geography first assumes the existence of shared interests along one dimension, an error that feminist intersectionality scholars elucidate (as well as feminist identity theorists, as discussed in Chapter 4). Second, geographic districting separates potential allies from one another. Guinier uses the separation of blacks from white allies as an example, but there are other sweeping issues, such as environmental concerns, which do not halt at district or state lines.

The controversy surrounding the Confederate flag atop the statehouse dome in Columbia, South Carolina, is a specific example of the potential for mass mobilization by coalition when issues of inclusive citizenship are at stake.

While the anti-flag coalition had allies from outside the state, it was initially quite easy for South Carolinians, and even national candidates such as George W. Bush and John McCain, to claim that this was an issue for South Carolinians to solve. This kind of response became less and less tenable as anti-flag activists transformed

> the issue from one of anti-confederacy and anti-racism to a frame of inclusive citizenship [which] widened acceptance for the anti-flag movement by linking the flag to issues of simple decent human treatment … It is clear … that the anti-flag forces in South Carolina encountered significant opposition. The power of the status quo, combined with citizen inertia, quiescence, and resignation kept the flag issue off the political agenda for decades … [T]he increased political power of African American citizens in South Carolina state government, a shift in the scope of the conflict from provincial concern to a national political audience, pressure from business interests, and the articulation of a universalistic frame of citizenship and sovereignty mobilized power to move the flag. (Woliver, Ledford, and Dolan 2001, 708–709)

It was the conscious move on the part of the anti-flag opposition to expand the meaning and scope of this debate beyond a racial or geographic concern that ultimately brought the other factors together (such as the tourism boycott by the National Association for the Advancement of Colored People (NAACP)) to relocate the flag at the Confederate Memorial on the statehouse grounds (not the optimal outcome for the anti-flag forces, but far superior to its previous location atop the dome as an official symbol of the state).

We are and have been, in fact, representing interests. The debate about whether or not we should be representing groups or individuals is thus a distraction, Guinier argues. A central issue revolves around *how* to go about representing interests in a way that maximizes the value of each vote. In an interesting test of Guinier's approach, Michael Suk-Young Chwe uses

> Condorcet's information aggregation model to show that sometimes the best decision procedure for the majority allows the minority to 'enforce' its favored outcome even when overruled by a majority. 'Special' voting power gives the minority an incentive to participate meaningfully, and more participation means more information is aggregated, which makes the majority better off. This result can be understood as a mathematical corroboration of Lani Guinier's arguments that voting procedures can be designed to encourage minority participation, benefiting everyone. (Chwe 1999, 85)

Chwe concludes:

> The most obvious grounds for challenging exclusion and expanding participation is fairness. But perhaps it is not hopelessly idealistic to think in terms of social welfare; Condorcet's information aggregation model lets us do so mathematically. The idea of information aggregation, much more than merely a justification of majority rule, enables us to see democracy not only as the fair resolution of conflicting interests but also as a collective enterprise in which each person's participation benefits everyone else. (Chwe 1999, 93)

Mark Graber takes a rather different approach to Guinier's work on electoral reform. He criticizes Guinier for being too strong a democrat by advocating a voting scheme that is just as likely (if not more so) to empower Ku Klux Klan members as it is racial minorities (Graber 1996). Graber comes to this conclusion because he has a fundamental disagreement with Guinier over the concept of representation. While Guinier refers to her work as in the spirit of James Madison, Graber balks. Madison, on Graber's account, leaned much more in the direction of understanding the representative as a trustee—emboldened and legitimized by the electorate to deliberate and employ prudent judgment. Guinier, on the other hand, prefers the delegate model of representation whereby the representative is more tightly linked to constituents and bound by their preferences.

The primary problem with Guinier's argument, for Graber, is that those preferences are just as likely to be anti-democratic, ethically repugnant, patently unfair, or all three. The delegate model, while highly democratic procedurally, can and probably will lead to undemocratic outcomes. Instead of investing time and energy on "romantic conceptions of a people willing to implement the latest rage in critical (or whatever) studies," we would be better off placing our trust, specifically, in the courts, where disadvantaged groups have achieved their greatest successes and, more generally, in "those persons trained to deliberate on matters of public importance" (Graber 1996, 306–307).

Graber is mistaken in his criticism because it is based on two false dichotomies. The first is the division of representation into two models, trustee and delegate, where Guinier becomes the spokesperson for the first and Madison (and Graber) for the second. This division, as Graber discusses it, is not so neat for either Guinier or Madison. As Pitkin (1967) points out, conceptions of representation are more like plots on a spectrum than either/or, mutually exclusive categories. Guinier believes that an important part of the problem of under-representation arises from the very lack of influence and accountability over who our representatives are *and* what they do while in office. In empowering marginalized groups through an electoral scheme that makes it more likely that the members of those groups will be able to elect representatives of their choosing, Guinier is supporting her vision of fair representation where all members of the polity should have equal access and influence over agendas and deliberations, the outcomes to which all members will be subject.

Guinier recognizes that representation never simply means strictly conveying the preferences of one's constituents without deviation to the legislative body. This is hardly representation, again to invoke Pitkin (as Guinier often does in precisely this context), since representation means something entirely different than simply transporting preferences. Representatives for Guinier should be responsible to their constituents, reflecting their interests (on which basis they were elected) and providing justifications when the representative's decisions run counter to those held by some constituents. Guinier is clearly aware that representatives cannot and should not simply be the mouthpieces of the represented—it is neither possible nor preferable. For Guinier the important thing is for the members of a democratic community to have equal influence over who will do the representing, where the judgment of how well it is done will be decided in the next election.

This brings us to the second false dichotomy Graber implies between the legislature and other rights-promoting bodies, such as the courts, as the proper site for effective remedy of inequality. By advocating electoral reform for choosing the members of the legislature, Guinier is hardly making a case for the irrelevancy of other decision making bodies. In fact, Guinier is quite cognizant of the influence (both for good and ill) of the courts in particular. She is not, in the larger scheme of things, opting for one at the expense of the other, but for one (and maybe an improved one) *in addition to* the other.

However Graber is clearly correct in asserting that some citizens hold opinions that run counter to the "politically inefficacious progressive persons of color", such as "more Americans believe that 'present policies unduly favor blacks than think present policy favors whites,' and approximately half of the citizenry believes that 'we have gone too far in pushing equal rights in this country'" (Graber 1996, 296). However, to use these surveys of voter attitudes as evidence that more "white reactionaries" will be elected by the electoral scheme meant to enhance under-represented racial minorities is not convincing. In fact this raises an important difference between what I want to advance and what Guinier proposes. I respond to Graber by arguing that the existence of these beliefs has historically been (and continues to be) translated into seats in the legislature. In fact, it is precisely the existence of these attitudes that requires a solution that truly takes into account social difference.

To take social difference seriously means that race or difference-blind electoral reform will not be enough to usher in meaningful change. What is more likely to foment such change is a public commitment to fund historically under-represented social groups for the purposes of mobilization and control of candidate slates. The groups that qualify are those who can demonstrate a history of disenfranchisement and marginalization, the present effects of which manifest themselves in poor showings on indicators of social well-being such as physical health, quality education, wealth, good jobs, home ownership, and personal safety.

This response would probably not satisfy Graber, since his overall thrust is hostile to group-specific remedies altogether, although he finds Guinier's race-blind semi-proportional system, informed by a desire to invigorate under-represented racial minorities, just as problematic. However, to claim that altering the electoral system in an effort to promote greater inclusiveness means creating more spaces for those with whom we vehemently disagree, as well as those with whom we agree, is a problem of democracy more generally. This criticism fails to recognize that what he fears in many ways already exists if the erosion of Affirmative Action, attrition of entitlements, and targeting of provisions such as Title IX are any indication. More inclusivity is needed.

Although I think Guinier is right to illustrate the group character of interests and, in some ways more importantly for my purposes, the fact that we are already attempting to represent group interests in the American electoral system, she pays too little attention in this earlier work to forms of political participation other than voting, and neglects the ways in which informal group recognition can increase more robust forms of political participation, thereby increasing the quality of representation, while preventing the further entrenchment and re-inscription of discriminatory practices and avoiding the problem of intra-group difference.

Political Race and the Possibilities for Coalition Politics

Guinier's newest work with Gerald Torres, *The Miner's Canary* (2002), begins to explore, among other things, participation beyond voting. The central aim is to provide an answer to the deficiencies of much of traditional identity politics scholarship, which Guinier and Torres argue tends to understand or treat race as a biological category. Although Guinier and Torres do not describe this body of work in so many words, the implication is that too much of it is unintentionally essentialist. In attempting to highlight the experiences of marginalization, many identity scholars began to emphasize particularity—the idea that the experience of oppression, and thus efforts to dismantle it, will be different for those along particular identity axes. What Guinier and Torres *do* emphasize at great length, however, are the ways in which this treatment of identity cordons off potential allies from one another and inhibits, if not practically prohibits, the formation of broad coalitions comprising those who have been *politically raced*.

Political race is the concept or device Guinier and Torres develop as a way to foment cooperation and more robust participation by the historically marginalized—with the primary emphasis on race but with some consideration of class. Political race is argued to be a highly revealing and powerful lens through which to identify systemic oppression and foster politically and socially powerful coalitions. It covers three elements: diagnostic, aspirational, and activist (Guinier and Torres 2002, 13). It is diagnostic in that it "offers a method of analysis to signal systemic failure and to catalyze institutional innovation" (Guinier and Torres 2002, 15).

Race, they point out, is a political construction as well as a social one. Racing is a practice of naming the powerless and reinscribing the power of privilege in a game in which the rules have already been made—and those rules are based on a zero-sum conception of power. Like the canary who alerts the miner when the environment has become toxic, political race enables us to identify systemic injustices perpetrated against people of color as well as poor whites. "Political race is not a theory of racial group membership, skin color, or other individual attributes traditionally associated with race. Instead, political race identifies a specific form of public meaning that is tied to the distribution of social goods and is thus intrinsically political. Race both reinforces hierarchies of power and, simultaneously, camouflages those hierarchies" (Guinier and Torres 2002, 16).

The aspirational and activist elements of this race project seek to enhance citizens' ability to see their fates as linked and thus more likely to engage in collective action. "Race becomes political in the sense of generating collective action only when it motivates people to connect their individual experiences to the experiences of others and then to act collectively in response to those experiences" (Guinier and Torres 2002, 17). As another scholar describes the concept,

> [t]heir concept of *political race* is cognizant of the personal dimensions of race, but focuses strictly on political activism and coalition building in a post-civil rights era. Political race is not a description of people's lives; instead, it functions as an invitation to everyone, regardless of racial classification, to band together in a grass-roots political movement aimed at remedying a long list of social inequalities that we might not recognize

> as being connected to racial injustice. Race is therefore important, not as a coping device or source of pride, but because racial minorities, and blacks in particular, are the most obvious victims of farther-reaching, more intricate webs of social inequality. African Americans serve a diagnostic function: they are metaphorical canaries in the mine, signaling the health of the broader polity. In essence, political race seeks to overcome the obstacle of racial self-interest. In lieu of liberalism's top-down, oppressor-victim model of power, Guinier and Torres opt for Michel Foucault's formulation of power as a vast, historically dependent maze that implicates everyone in the perpetuation of social hierarchies. We fail to notice that 'race camouflages unfair resource distribution among whites as well as blacks' (20). (Fogg-Davis 2003, 560)

Political race is thus superior to what Guinier and Torres call "cosmetic diversity." Diversity understood in terms of biology or skin color falls short, they argue, in at least four ways. First, it reinforces the idea that change can be achieved by a few committed individuals working within existing institutions. "This strategy supports the idea that individual success is the best measure of reform. A more thoroughgoing institutional critique never gets off the ground" (Guinier and Torres 2002, 129). Second, once outsiders are incorporated into the existing hierarchy, their ability to confront the fundamental organization of that hierarchy is seriously compromised, and "once a space is made for critics within the dominant institutions, any failure to deliver substantive goods is not a failure of the institution but their own personal failure. External critics are encouraged to blame the internal players; the community from which the critics emerged is demoralized" (Guinier and Torres 2002, 129). Third, the incorporation of a few outsiders (even if compelled by a mass movement) inhibits the creation and growth of critical spaces for resistance. "For resistance to emerge that has the strength to construct competing metanarratives and sustain critique, it must have a space for democratic, economic, and critical social experimentation" (Guinier and Torres 2002, 130). Finally, "strategies of cosmetic diversity pit potential allies against one another" (Guinier and Torres 2002, 130). So long as we continue to divide along racial lines and thus refuse to recognize the systemic nature of the injustices that affect people of color as well as poor whites, fundamental institutional change is unlikely to occur. These divisions encourage participation in a blame game that serves to buttress the status quo.

Political Race/Political Identity?

Nevertheless, the political race concept remains underdeveloped. I think this is primarily so for three key and related reasons. The first is that, in many instances, the scope of Guinier and Torres remains limited to legal decisions surrounding districting, gerrymandering, and voting. The second is that the omission of gender from consideration in the concept of political race hinders its capacity to generate the kind of coalition formation and participation necessary to develop alternative representational schemes. The third is that a recognition of the connected and interlocking nature of racial and class injustice is not likely to occur without some already existing, fairly robust political participation that brings members of these groups together to demonstrate such links. Yet even if those linkages can be established prior to increased political engagement, recognition of a linked fate or condition is not likely to be enough to *initiate* political participation in a broad and sustained fashion for the bulk of members of disadvantaged groups.

While Guinier and Torres claim to be offering solutions that go beyond the legal and historical basis of political representation, most of the examples they employ to illustrate political race in action rely on either a (top-down) court decision or activism that is somewhat successful but ultimately falls back upon redrawing district lines more favorable to the disadvantaged. The successes they point to indicate that there is surely worth in the concept of political race. My concern is that its reach is bounded. The few examples that do not fall into one of these two categories are limited by the second reason wherein gender assumes virtually no role in the concept of political race. The following excerpt seeks to justify the omission of gender:

> It may be that those who are thrust together by their experience of being raced will act first and lead. Indeed, it is probably critical for people of color to lead this movement. But it is equally critical that they find allies if a movement for social justice, and not just for racial justice, is to succeed. In this way, political race is similar to feminism; it may be more likely that women consider themselves feminists and lead the struggle for gender equality, but there is nothing about the term feminism that excludes men from also claiming the form of analysis and critique it embraces. *Political race has the potential to be an even more transformative force than conventional feminism, however, because it seeks to use the experiences of people of color as the basis for fundamental social change that will benefit not only blacks and Hispanics but other disadvantaged social groups.* (Guinier and Torres 2002, 20–21; emphasis mine)

This passage is, in many ways, essentially correct. We should look to the lived experiences of citizens—especially those who have been historically marginalized—to craft fairer and more democratic policies and practices. I think this is what Guinier and Torres mean by the comparison with feminism; feminist scholarship and activism were and continue to be an outgrowth of the ways in which supposedly universal and objective norms and procedures harm the life chances of the least advantaged. Guinier and Torres would probably argue, however, with my use of the phrase "least advantaged" in this context but would find it acceptable if I were to substitute "women." The emphasized portion of the above passage stresses that political race is potentially more transformative than "conventional feminism"; political race centers analysis in such a way that it will produce broader and more thoroughgoing change. If by "conventional feminism" Guinier and Torres mean early feminist scholarship, then they are correct. If they mean contemporary, mainstream liberal feminism, which is more likely, then there is some, though limited, evidence for their claim.

In either instance, however, this is a fairly weak argument. Most of the ideas that Guinier and Torres employ in an effort to create an alternative (non-biological, non-essentialist) basis for collective action and inclusion actually hail from feminist theory. Furthermore, the vast majority of contemporary feminist thought does not simply focus upon inquiry into the nature of gender in social life. Rather it works from shifting axes. Given particular circumstances, one's race, gender, sexuality, or class might be the most powerful lens through which to diagnose systemic injustice. Given the history of slavery in the United States, race assumes a uniquely powerful position for indicating systems of injustice. Yet how those systems operate is always context-specific and, when viewed through only one lens, can mask intra-group marginality. Some of the most robust feminist scholarship that has been done (and continues to be done) argues that oppressive relations can best be viewed and transformed at the intersections of race, class, gender, sexuality, age, and disability. For example, Kimberlé Crenshaw writes, "the failure to embrace the complexities of compoundedness is not simply a matter of political will, but it is also due to the influence of a way of thinking about discrimination which structures politics so that struggles are categorized as singular issues. Moreover, this structure imports a descriptive and normative view of society that reinforces the status quo" (Crenshaw 1998, 394; see also Crenshaw 1995; hooks 1990, 2000; and Weber 2001).

Much later in the book, Guinier and Torres return to their omission of gender.

> We have chosen, however, not to stress the link between gender and power, although it is a potentially important site of struggle. We certainly invite others to explore it further. Indeed, we believe that a richer discussion of political race would incorporate more research on issues of gender. Gender is a strong lens for viewing manifestations of disempowerment or disengagement. But it needs to be linked to race or class if the perceived unfairness is to generate a public willingness to act collectively. (Guinier and Torres 2002, 163)

Again, there is nothing much to disagree with here, except for the fact that there is a fairly substantial body of feminist literature that incorporates not only race, gender, and class but sexuality as well. They never engage with this literature, which is surprising given that much of it seems only to bolster one of their primary (and convincing) arguments that it is necessary to recognize the interconnections among those who have been historically marginalized and how those ties can serve as a potentially powerful site for collective action.

The final passage in the book confronts this issue of putting gender to the side. They maintain that, despite what we have learned about the importance of linking race, gender, and class, gender remains primarily associated with the claims of middle- and upper-class women. As a result, gender, much more so than race, has been the means for exploiting rather than challenging the hierarchy. Thus white women have enjoyed "unprecedented upward mobility" (Guinier and Torres 2002, 166). Being cognizant of gender inequality alone, Guinier and Torres continue, has not moved us toward the construction of a collective and oppositional consciousness necessary to challenge structures of power. "Unless it is linked to race," they explain, "gender may be less helpful as the primary engine of transformative political mobilization, although it offers much on which to build ... But it is often less effective in identifying structures of public power ... We have chosen in this book to focus on race" (Guinier and Torres 2002, 166). They conclude their defense by pointing out that by focusing on race "we are simultaneously pushing for a more inclusive concept of power, so that whoever exercises it does so with different goals and more democratic practices" (Guinier and Torres 2002, 166).

Once again, I think there is little doubt that gender alone cannot serve as the means by which to diagnose and dismantle oppressive systems of power. There are very few, if any, contemporary feminist theorists that would attempt to make that claim. Furthermore, Guinier and Torres never cite evidence to support their claim that Affirmative Action has benefited white women much more than people of color. Their point is well-taken, however, that racializing Affirmative Action is a powerful tactic for attempting to shore up greater antagonism against it. Yet using political race as the lens for identifying systemic oppression reveals three problems with their overall thesis, each of which builds on the other.

The first is that the statement would be correct if qualified. White women have benefited from Affirmative Action *at the macro level* much more so than people of color. So long as the field is not one that remains overwhelmingly understood as "male," white women have indeed benefited from Affirmative Action at higher rates than people of color. However, when Affirmative Action is tracked by profession, being male can work in one's favor much more so than one's race, particularly in male-dominated professions such as law enforcement and construction/trades (Murrell and Jones 1996).

Furthermore, Lynn Weber's development of a conceptual framework for identifying and understanding the intersections of race, class, gender, and sexuality skillfully demonstrates the multiple, simultaneous, and insidious ways in which systems of power operate. She recounts the story (told originally to Studs Terkel) of Margaret Welch, a white single mother of two, who moved to Chicago from Tennessee after the death of her first husband. When her second husband left her, Margaret was forced to go on public aid. Through a public assistance program, Margaret obtained a scholarship to pursue a nursing degree. After successful completion of her first year of courses, however, the financial aid office informed Margaret that the scholarship would no longer be available to her as it was designed to assist minority students, and enough Hispanics had applied. Margaret reacted with anger and confusion: "I feel like I've been robbed of a chance to finish school … I don't believe black people should be pushed back. But I don't feel because I'm white, I should be either. It goes both ways. I don't think the gap is that big on a street level, not in my neighborhood. But when you get into the bureaucracy, business, and school, it's those people making the noise" (Weber 2001, 62–3).

Margaret mostly saw her plight through the lens of race, which offers important but partial insights. "Class scholars would emphasize the way that ideas about and structures of economic class influence Margaret's life" (Weber 2001, 68). Gender scholars would highlight pay disparities between men and women in the labor market, and the social and psychological processes that structured Margaret's choice of a female-dominated profession that pays less and requires fewer years of education than male-dominated health professions (Weber 2001, 69).

Additionally, Margaret's heterosexuality can blind her (and others) to the privileges such a position can confer in a prescribed sexual hierarchy. "How would her story be different if Margaret decided to live with another women to make ends meet … would she be suspected of being a lesbian … what would happen if she were lesbian or bisexual … what are the processes through which heterosexuality is socially constructed and legally enforced as a prerequisite for being seen as a 'good mother'" (Weber 2001, 70)? Weber's framework powerfully indicates the complexity and interconnectedness of oppressive systems of power when viewed through multiple lenses.

The second problem is that the statements of Guinier and Torres about Affirmative Action seem to encourage divisiveness among those who have been historically excluded—a divisiveness that they are trying hard to diminish. Indeed they go on to state that gender, more so than race, has been a mechanism for infiltrating rather than attempting to dismantle hierarchy. No evidence is brought to bear in support of this statement nor examples provided to illustrate exactly what they have in mind. Nonetheless, it is a fairer statement that most policy and activism geared toward remedying race *and* gender discrimination has historically been incremental and rather accommodationist.

Finally, their statement, misleading and potentially divisive, points to the ways in which race—even political race—may not be the powerful lens Guinier and Torres think it is for fostering coalitions. Insofar as gender is left completely to the side, political race blinds us to the insidious ways in which gender, race, class, and sexuality intersect, and thus hinders our ability to identify potentially potent interventions.

Although political race enables the identification of instances of systemic injustice, insofar as it neglects gender, it can blind us to other such instances and limit the kind of cooperation Guinier and Torres so rightly value. There are many good reasons for using race (even "political" race) as the centerpiece for an analysis of so-called democratic practices and procedures. One is the privileging of American law in which there is a much firmer grounding for cases of race discrimination (for very good reasons) than there is for gender, especially given that anti-discrimination doctrine in the United States identifies race as a suspect class while gender is only quasi-suspect.

Kimberlé Crenshaw, for example, points out the problems that anti-discrimination legislation poses based on its uni-dimensionality of group recognition. She argues that the discrimination against black females is virtually erased by anti-discrimination doctrine as applied by the courts. In one of the three cases she uses to support her claim, *DeGraffenreid v. General Motors*, five black women brought suit against General Motors, alleging that "the employer's seniority system perpetuated the effects of past discrimination against black women" (Crenshaw 1998, 141). The district court granted summary judgment for the defendant, rejecting the plaintiffs' attempt to bring suit on behalf of *black women*. The court stated that the lawsuit must be examined "for race discrimination, sex discrimination, or alternatively either, but not a combination of both" (Crenshaw 1998, 141).

The point, as Crenshaw deftly illustrates, is that these women did not experience discrimination solely on the basis of either race or gender. Black men had a record of being promoted at General Motors, as had white women. Race discrimination cases, as she points out, tend to illustrate discrimination against *black men*, while gender discrimination cases more often highlight the experiences of *white women*. The experiences of black women are essentially erased. They were discriminated against on the basis of the particular intersection of their race and gender: not as women, not as black, but as *black women*. The courts are virtually impotent to remedy these kinds of cases, which again indicate subjectivity. In fact there is strong historical evidence that the courts have been highly problematic vehicles for change when it comes to women and minorities and that popular mobilization has been much more successful in this regard (Rosenberg 1993).

While Guinier and Torres state that their project is not specifically about political representation, they are clear that their hope is that politicizing race, or the identity of the historically marginalized, will provide a basis upon which new coalitions will be formed, citizens will feel a greater sense of efficacy, and political participation will increase, all of which should improve the representation of the poor and people of color. "Only when individuals freely join together to resist and transform the forces of conventional power which named them as part of a group in the first place can the possibilities emerge for generating new forms of collective and democratic struggle" (Guinier and Torres 2002, 18).

Indeed, "[g]roup identity motivates individuals to join a social movement. When their group identity becomes a political identity, people are more willing to participate in the group's activities, to identify with its practices, and to make sacrifices for its cohesion" (Guinier and Torres 2002, 80). Interestingly, they use the phrase "political identity," which seems to me a more inclusive and potentially powerful concept than political race. While their claim is clearly that people of color are among the most severely disenfranchised, and that by politicizing race we are better equipped to diagnose structural inequalities that affect multiple groups, I am not convinced that political race is as sensitive to the ways in which gender, class, and sexuality intersect that even a politicized conception of race cannot encompass.

Nevertheless, the examples that Guinier and Torres employ to exemplify why and how coalitions have formed between people of color and poor whites are compelling. One excellent example Guinier and Torres use relates to Affirmative Action and Texas education reform. In 1996 the Fifth Circuit court declared in *Hopwood v. Texas* that race-conscious admissions policies in higher education were unconstitutional. In an effort to forestall a re-segregation of institutions of higher education, sociologists, demographers, education experts, historians, lawyers, and representatives of such groups as the Mexican American Legal Defense Fund and the Texas NAACP convened a series of meetings to discuss and amass data on the state of education in Texas. From those discussions and analyses of the data, it became clear that it was not only African-American and Hispanic students that stood to lose in the aftermath of *Hopwood*, but poor and working-class white students "also lost out because the SAT and LSAT [which favors more privileged students who have access to prep courses and are exposed to a wider range of experiences] so influenced admission decisions" (Guinier and Torres 2002, 70). "After much arguing, the issue of race was finally joined to issues of class and democratic access to public education more generally. Race became a lens through which to focus on the way the university was admitting everyone" (Guinier and Torres 2002, 70).

Guinier and Torres then describe a fairly unified coalition that proposed a policy (subsequently adopted) that requires the flagship universities in the state of Texas to admit students who graduate in the top 10 percent of their high school, regardless of SAT scores. It is worth noting, however, that this "race-neutral" approach (an approach currently defended by the George W. Bush Administration in lieu of using race as one of many factors in admissions decisions) seriously divided the members of the original coalition. That division was characterized, on the one hand, by those who supported the "ten percent plan" as a way to at least maintain or even possibly increase the Affirmative Action-era enrollments of poor and working class minorities and women and those who were concerned about the unintended consequences of such a plan to encourage or reinforce secondary school segregation. This latter group argues that so-called race-neutral percentage plans like the ones in Texas, California, and Florida only provide diverse enrollments insofar as the secondary school systems remain racially and economically segregated. This is a matter of grave concern as a recent study conducted by the Civil Rights Project at Harvard University (2002) found that since 1986 there has been a nationwide trend toward re-segregation in the public schools, with the worst cases in the South and West. The most rapidly re-segregating districts are in Texas and Georgia, and three of the five whitest districts are in Texas.

I do not want to imply that race or even political race is not a powerful experience through which to diagnose the existence of systemic power. However, I do think that it will have the potential to block from consideration how women, gay men, and lesbians suffer in ways that political race might not accommodate. Guinier and Torres fail to provide examples of these groups forging coalitions with women, gay men, or lesbians. Under what circumstances would they do so?

Are there good reasons to believe that these coalitions might be more difficult to foster?

I wonder because, while people of color undoubtedly suffer some of the worst injustices, including blatantly racist practices, gay men and lesbians are still widely and openly regarded as immoral and depraved, by both whites and people of color. There remain widespread understandings that women, by their very nature, are unfit for certain occupations and lifestyles—even among certain so-called progressive groups. This is not to say that people of color do not hold similar beliefs. Rather it might be that it is more acceptable to hold such beliefs about women, gay men, and lesbians, and it makes me question how political race can accommodate these concerns. "For as groups vie for the label of legitimate, normal, and citizen, they confront the requirement that they regulate and control the public behavior and image of all group members, especially those perceived as nonconformist" (Cohen 1997, 575; see also Sullivan 1996). It is often the marginalization *within* disadvantaged groups that goes unrecognized. In fact there is a long and now well-documented history of the ways in which the concerns of women in the Civil Rights Movement and lesbians in the second wave of the women's movement were silenced in an effort to present a "united front" (McAdam 1982; Chong 1991; Costain 1992). Such concerns were not only regarded as divisive, but were understood to be quite secondary in nature. More recently Cathy Cohen noted that, "consistently, in nationwide public opinion surveys such as the American National Election Survey or the 1993–94 national Black Politics Survey, when respondents are asked to rank or rate groups, lesbians and gay men come last behind such categories as 'illegal aliens'" (Cohen 1997, 603).

In Cincinnati, one of the most segregated cities in the United States, which has in recent years experienced serious racial strife, a human rights ordinance was proposed in 1992 that included "protection against discrimination on the basis of, among other factors, H.I.V. status, sexual orientation, or 'Appalachian regional origin'" (Singer 2002, 46). The leading gay rights group in Cincinnati, Stonewall Cincinnati, was foremost in lobbying the City Council to pass the ordinance. The ordinance was eliminated the following year, however, when voters approved a city charter revision (Article 12) by a two-to-one margin that "specifically prohibited the city from enforcing the human-rights ordinance on behalf of gay men and bisexuals and forbade the council to pass any future gay rights legislation" (Singer 2002, 46). One of the most prominent supporters of Article 12 was a black minister, K.Z. Smith. The rallying cry became "Equal Rights, Not Special Rights," and Reverend Smith's wife appeared in a widely aired television spot saying, "Some people say that homosexual behavior is the same as being black. Does anyone really believe that? This makes no sense to me. We need to stop this in Cincinnati. I'm voting 'Yes'" (Singer 2002, 46).

With regard to social class, Hèctor G. Bladuell writes that

> Guinier and Torres's discussion of the racial bribe [the opportunity to be integrated into the dominant white culture provided they leave behind their indigenous roots] downplays the relevance of class in minority group dynamics. They do not consider seriously the fact that the bribe to 'become White' is opened to Blacks and other minority groups that move up the economic ladder and dissociate themselves with Black culture and political identity. In other words, the racial bribe is not only open to minorities that are lighter skinned but, in many instances, is open to minorities who can pay their way into 'Whiteness.' Class is as important as, or more important than, skin pigmentation is assessing who is offered the racial bribe. (Bladuell 2001/2002, 139)

Bladuell makes a further point about the racial bribe:

> Discussion of the racial bribe among Latinos also leaves out the distinction between involuntary and voluntary minorities. Voluntary minorities, mainly immigrants and first-generation citizens, are less concerned about their disadvantaged position in society than involuntary minorities, mainly second and further generations, because they often compare their position in the United States to their position in their home country and prefer the former. On the other hand, involuntary minorities tend to resist assimilation and tend to fight against their subordinate status in society. Therefore, voluntary minorities have a different cultural frame of reference than involuntary minorities, who develop an 'oppositional culture.' Many voluntary minorities do not associate with Blacks and Latinos who are involuntary minorities because they do not share their cultural frame of reference. However, not associating with the struggle of involuntary minorities is different from assimilating and 'becoming White.' Guinier and Torres's analysis of the racial bribe would have been more complete if this distinction was addressed. (Bladuell 2001/2002, 139)

It is not that I think coalitions of diverse groups are impossible or even improbable. Guinier and Torres leave unanswered how truly diverse coalitions might arise. I think they actually do want to politicize *identity* altogether, but remain curiously wedded to this idea of political race. To be sure, they point to successful collective action based on a politicized conception of race. My point is that, while these successes demonstrate the value of conceiving difference in such a way, mobilization ignited on this basis will probably be bounded by the parameters of the concept itself. That is, by spotlighting race and class, political race masks the ways in which gender and sexuality do not just intersect with race and class, but at those intersections the very meanings of racial and class differences change. Insofar as political race neglects these concerns, participants can be blinded to the gendered character of race and class such that grassroots mobilization across relevant differences is narrowed and compromised.

Of course the geographic districting that Guinier criticized in her earlier work still threatens to limit the possibilities for coalition formation. Guinier's overall vision of representation seeks first to shift the understanding of ourselves from one of radical individualism to one where we refuse to regard our existence as unique and isolated. Second Guinier urges us to *recognize* that our position as a member of a particular race and/or class is also not distinctive insofar as other groups share in this larger disenfranchisement that systemically privileges the few over the many.

Finally, the third reason Guinier and Torres's concept of political race is underdeveloped is that diagnosing systemic inequality through the lens of race and revealing the ways in which racial inequality is linked to and reinforced by other structured inequalities is not enough to initiate the kind of political participation I assert is necessary to infuse representation with real political power. There is a substantial body of social movement literature that makes it clear that something like "cognitive liberation," to use Doug McAdam's terminology, or identifying certain kinds of treatment as not simply individualized and private but targeted at broader groupings, causing negative social and political consequences, is a necessary but not sufficient generator of collective political activity (see especially Costain 1992; McAdam 1982; Tarrow 1998; and Tilly 2003).

Doug McAdam's study of the American civil rights movement, Anne Costain's analysis of second-wave feminism, Sidney Tarrow's cross-national examination of the rise and fall of cycles of contention, and Charles Tilly's scholarship on the general processes that contribute to waves of collective violence across the globe all agree that some level of dissatisfaction or deprivation must exist for collective activity to ensue. However, movement cycles do not correspond with any regularity with increased levels of discontent. Instead, phases of collective political action tend to arise when outrage is joined with the availability of external resources (particularly financial resources), the cultivation of internal resources (especially a web-like organizational structure that connects core participants to the periphery), and the opening of political opportunities that signal a receptivity within power structures to the kinds of claims movements make.

Some level of social dissatisfaction can be expected to exist at all times, and if the scholarship mentioned above tells us anything, it is that no amount of discontent alone is likely to *initiate* collective action. In fact, these same studies also demonstrate that a recognition of injustice or linked fate is likely not to come about prior to organization but after. Thus in order to initiate political participation, we must provide incentives for marginalized citizens to act on their outrage. Providing public funding for the organization of historically disadvantaged groups would go a significant way toward funneling passion into action. This prescription will be picked up in more depth in Chapter 5.

Conclusion

Guinier wants to improve the representation of historically disadvantaged groups by altering the electoral system such that votes cast are more likely to be counted toward the election of a preferred candidate arising from multi-member rather than single-member districts. Yet for electoral reform to have any real bite, she recognizes, and I wholeheartedly agree, that there must be some basis upon which we can encourage and facilitate greater political participation precisely from these communities of interest. Without increased participation from under-represented groups, electoral reform becomes like the elaborate party no one came to.

For Guinier and Torres, members of historically marginalized groups will be more likely to engage in collective action when they are able to recognize how inequality structures their lives in ways not fully captured by individual choice. This recognition also entails laying bare how race and class intersect in powerful ways to perpetuate oppression, providing a natural basis upon which to found a coalition of blacks and poor and working class whites.

Such is the concept of political race: it is the miner's canary that alerts us to danger (the existence of systemic inequality) initially through the lens of race, a most powerful lens because of the American legacy of slavery. Following the initial diagnosis, we can more effectively unmask the structural economic inequality (something we are particularly loath to perceive much less discuss openly in the United States) that reaches across class lines but masquerades quite effectively as the outcome of fair and equal opportunities.

This is group representation in the weak sense: informal recognition of groups insofar as interests are a social concept. However, does this informal recognition go far enough, and is the representation of *interests* too partial, limiting the possibilities for cooperation and a larger vision of well-being or even justice?

Guinier's most insightful contributions to this representation dilemma are significant. She points out the ways in which we are already representing groups, although the proxy for interests is presently geography. In fact, representation is always about groups and degrees of exclusion (those that are in one group or a series of groups, and those that are not). The central questions ought to be about the best way(s) to alter the electoral system to facilitate the representation of interests while providing incentives for increased participation and coalition-building across geographic and other cleavage lines in order to foster the inclusion of all relevant groups. In the next chapter I will show that Anne Phillips, similar to Guinier, rejects any formal recognition of marginalized "groups" because of the ways in which identity (and thus interests) crosscuts traditional divisions along the lines of race, ethnicity, class, gender and sexuality. The cross-cutting nature of identity and interests then renders the entire project of establishing which groups should count virtually impossible. Part of what makes Phillips's work so valuable is the seriousness she attaches to these issues of intra-group difference. For while Guinier and Phillips generally agree on why a robust form of group representation is not advisable, Anne Phillips provides a sustained argument of the potential pitfalls.

My primary criticisms of Guinier do not reside with her prescriptions for electoral reform. Such reform is what I find most appealing about her work. Nor am I troubled by her emphasis on the connection between political representation and participation. In fact, I too want to make just such a connection. The disagreement comes in how best to procure or initiate the participation necessary to make electoral reform worthwhile. Guinier's and Torres's political race concept does much to help diagnose structural inequality based on race and class. However, it is, first, insufficiently inclusive to envelop inequality based on gender and sexuality. Second, as a large and expanding literature on collective political action makes clear, acknowledgment of injustice and the existence of natural allies, while important, are generally not enough to instigate the kind of broad-based political participation necessary for electoral reform to deliver meaningful results. Ironically, the concept of political race could be put to use in a way that Guinier and Torres do not adequately notice: as a way of identifying not only instances of systemic inequality but also as a means for demonstrating why some groups can be justifiably singled out for additional representational scrutiny given built-in disadvantages. As further discussed in Chapter 4, political race might then be a valuable and complementary addition to Iris Young's defense of the representation of "structural groups."

Chapter 3

Feminism and Democracy: Anne Phillips and the Politics of Equality

> Classifications, and the very notion of social class, would not be such a decisive stake in struggle (among the classes) if they did not contribute to the existence of the social classes, enhancing the efficacy of the objective mechanisms that determine the distributions and ensure their reproduction, by adding to them the consent of the minds which they structure. The object of social science is a reality that encompasses all the individual and collective struggles aimed at conserving or transforming reality, in particular, those that seek to impose the legitimate definition of reality, whose specifically symbolic efficacy can help to conserve or subvert the established order, that is to say, reality. (Bourdieu 1990, 141)

> Those who are increasingly feeling the brunt of the decisions of this administration look like us here in this church. They don't look like the Congress or the staff at the White House or, for that matter, even the Supreme Court. Which is another cause for alarm. It appears that America's poor and people of color are the **cannon-fodder** for Bush's New American Century. (Cynthia McKinney, US Representative, GA 2002)

While the law can be a powerful resource as well as a restrictive cell, it works best when it is being formulated, interpreted, and applied by a representative body that reflects relevant interests as well as mirroring the racial, ethnic, gender, and cultural makeup of the polity. This statement captures much of Anne Phillips's project.

Speaking about feminist democratic theory may seem somewhat repetitive given that a commitment to feminism entails a fundamental commitment to democracy. This commitment is fundamental because, while feminist theory captures a variety of approaches and values, not all of which are commensurable with one another, it remains coherent methodologically and substantively insofar as it (1) regards gender, race, ethnicity, class, and sexuality as powerful forces that inform, structure, and legitimize the social order, and (2) advances democratic and egalitarian measures as the only justifiable means for rectifying inequality. Of course, feminists will continue to disagree about just how and to what degree social difference conditions social reality and what manner of democratic intervention is required. Nevertheless feminism, attuned to the exercise of power, is fundamentally committed to democracy as the only egalitarian, fair, and legitimate means for arriving at decisions under which all members of a polity must live. Thus all feminists are democrats of some stripe.

However for Anne Phillips, equality takes pride of place. Charles Tilly concurs by stating that "justice, in her [Phillips's] text, consists almost entirely of equal treatment" (Tilly 2001, 131). Equal treatment, for Phillips, requires that relevant social differences figure into the ways we institutionalize political representation.

Is There Any Such Thing as a "Group"?

Phillips is concerned, like all of the scholars under review here, with increasing the inclusiveness of the polity and asks whether or not political equality can be meaningful without formal mechanisms for representing group difference. On her account, similar to Guinier, we must reject "group representation," understood by her to mean groups differentiated on the basis of some ascriptive characteristic (race, gender, ethnicity, sexuality), which can then only be represented by a member of that particular group. We must reject this potential remedy because of the host of problems it carries with it. Group representation solidifies difference by making judgments about what the relevant differences are, and those differences, absent plausible mechanisms for determining relevance, are likely not to reflect what the majority of their members regard as determinative or important. This is the unattractive and dangerous essentialist turn that group representation entails, according to Phillips.

By making a judgment about what differences matter, we are necessarily making some claim about the shared concerns or interests of particular groups based solely on their membership in some identity category. For example, that all African Americans support Affirmative Action and all women are pro-choice are statements that are clearly not true and render the notion that identity groups can be represented incoherent. Individuals have cross-cutting group memberships. One can be female, wealthy, and a lesbian, and it is virtually impossible to ascertain not only what aspects of one's identity will be more or less decisive for informing one's interests or policy positions, but also how one understands what it even means to be "female," "wealthy," and "lesbian." I can equally imagine such a citizen claiming, for example, that "because I am female, I am pro-choice," and "because I am female, I am pro-life."

All of these concerns, Phillips argues, contribute to an unacceptable understanding of accountability in representation. Like Pitkin's concern about "mirror representation," Phillips points out that it becomes virtually impossible to speak about holding a representative accountable if there is no agreed upon set of issues, concerns, and positions that a representative is to pursue, something we cannot expect of groups partitioned in such a way. If we value equality, according to Phillips, then the group representation solution may very well be worse than the original dilemma.

Instead, we must "say that the people marked by particular group characteristics are under-represented (not then the group but those bearing group characteristics), and that we need to elect more representative who share the markers and experiences of that group" (Phillips 1999, 40). In this way we should adopt a system of proportional representation (this in the case of women) within multi-member districts and party lists that require quotas based upon (at a minimum) gender and ethnicity. To be clear, Phillips is not arguing for reserved seats for these groups. She explicitly rejects this proposal. Rather she calls for a quota system at the party list stage to ensure that women and members of under-represented ethnic groups have a more equal opportunity of being elected. Such programs, she points out, have been quite successful in a number of European countries which can boast that women comprise up to 34% of their legislatures—a significant improvement on the roughly 14% claimed by the United States and the UK.

Yet party list quotas, she maintains, must be distinguished from a robust notion of group representation. "Though feminists have employed a variety of arguments in pressing the case for political quotas, the crucial one does not—and I believe should not—rest on a notion of group representation. More than anything, it is an argument in terms of political equality" (Phillips 1993, 99). That voices are being silenced cannot be improved, she argues, by group representation; in fact such a move actually weakens the argument. "Accountability is always the other side of representation and, in the absence of procedures for establishing what any group wants or thinks, we cannot usefully talk of their political representation" (Phillips 1993, 99).

However if Guinier is right, and I think she is, about how we already engage in a form of group representation in the United States based on geographic districting, then the question turns upon how best to go about defining and representing groups. It is certainly true, as Guinier points out, that "group representation" based on single-member geographic districting might not be preferable to other schemes. Nevertheless, we have been usefully talking about and acting upon (with varying degrees of success) representational questions such as districting and accountability for a good many decades. Phillips clearly wants to make the argument that group representation in the strong sense (the special representation of identity groups by only those that share those characteristics) tends to leave open some uncomfortable and particularly difficult questions about just *how* one can really speak about representing a race, culture, or gender. Furthermore, the possible (and some actual) responses to such queries are generally less likely to foster better representation and actually be more oppressive of the group than if there were no special representation rights at all. Yet political representation always entails a depiction, reflection, or illustration of some group of people. The questions we keep returning to, however, are how best to define the "who" (Who is being represented?) so that there will be some clues as to the "how" (What practices, processes, and institutions should we adopt for the fair representation of this group?).

Phillips calls for gender quotas at the party list stage precisely because women, compared with other disadvantaged groups, form the least cohesive of "groups," yet they are clearly marked in ways that remain less clear for race and ethnicity. In other words, unlike blacks (and to a lesser degree Latinos), we cannot say anything about the political preferences of "women." Of course we cannot make proclamations about any unified positions of blacks, but given the shared experience of slavery and its legacy of thoroughgoing institutional racism, there are likely to be some shared interests based upon experience that cannot be said about the experiences of women (as a group). Requiring gender quotas at the party list stage helps to negotiate the equal concern Phillips has with the necessity of both a politics of presence and a politics of ideas. Such quotas would probably lend themselves to the increased presence of women in legislative bodies (signaling an erosion of structural inequalities) thereby paving the way for a more inclusive and robust politics of ideas—while not coming to any conclusions about what those ideas would be. This proposal, Phillips argues, escapes the "implausible essentialism that sees shared experience as enough of a guarantee of shared belief and avoids the unlikely possibility that some "sufficiently representative segment" could be organized to "establish group opinions and goals" (Phillips 1995, 55).

Yet what is "implausible" and "essentialist" about the claim that shared experiences are likely to affect and condition interests in important ways? Surely there is never any "guarantee" of what *precisely* those interests will be (but neither is there any requirement to make such narrow predictions). The kind of claim I want to defend in this project is that experiences of race, gender, sexuality, ethnicity, and class are particularly powerful structural forces in the American context, the effects of which we can readily observe by the notable deficit of women, minorities, and the poor among those achieving the good things in life (e.g. meaningful, dignified jobs, educational achievement, and physical health). Yet those same groups tend to be over-represented in measures of social marginality (unemployment, disease, and incarceration, for example).

While the experiences of gender differ in important ways from that of race, there are some things we can say about gender as a category. In fact, it is these group categories that give meaning to this whole conversation about increasing the representation of disadvantaged groups. The problem, of course, is whether or not there are any acceptable ways to enhance the opportunities of such groups to influence policy. Phillips is right to point to the necessity of avoiding essentialism that narrowly equates experience with belief. Although she is correct to point to the difficulties posed by measures such as public funding to aid in the organization of disadvantaged groups, she is too quick to dismiss the likelihood of group organization to ascertain and advance group interests. These difficulties include how to go about establishing which groups would qualify for special treatment. Even if we could settle the first question, it quickly begs another: could the relevant groups be organized in such a way as to reflect the diversity *within* the groups?

Gender Convergence and Political Equality

In the case of gender, Phillips advances convergence as one of the primary means for fostering greater equity. For Phillips, fundamental change in gender relations depends on a convergence of the "female" and "male." She explains, "I would say it is hard to maintain the conviction of equal worth for both sexes when women and men are segregated into different occupations and expected to act such different parts in their social and domestic lives. Sexual equality, in my view, does depend on convergence" (Phillips 1999, 94). In fact "[c]onvergence, understood as a transformation in the conditions of life for both women *and* men, is not objectionable" (Phillips 1999, 94). It is not objectionable for Phillips since "female" only has meaning in relation to "male."

However, is this true? Furthermore, do we want such a convergence or androgyny? Might that simply establish a new paradigm of genderlessness, the deviation from which brings punishments? That it would be okay for "men" to be more like "women" and vice versa seems appealing, but either sex conforming too closely to their respective gender extremes would presumably be unacceptable (and possibly understood to be suffering from false consciousness). This call to convergence could be just as dangerous as the freezing of gender differences—it is just freezing of a different sort (where the norm is androgyny). As discussed in Chapter 1, our experience with neutrality of gender "blindness" has often reinforced the privileges of the dominant or "normal" gender.

Of course, convergence is only appropriate to some differences, gender being a case in point. Racial and ethnic identities, Phillips is careful to point out, probably are not appropriate sites for convergence. However, I wonder how we then deal with cross-cutting memberships under her theory of convergence (i.e. black women). Being a black female means something different, socially and culturally, than being a white woman. Phillips could be read here, although this is certainly not her intention, as advocating convergence to a white female norm—especially given that she does not specify what "convergence" would look like for those who possess multiple differences (e.g. see Collins 2000, Chapter 4).

There is a precarious balance Phillips wants to strike between group considerations and individual preferences. In fact, she prefers to err in the direction of individual preferences (which is why she sees party list quotas not as a form of group representation but as a measure aimed at increasing the cache of relevant ideas and preferences). If we need both greater inclusion of members of historically disadvantaged groups as well as the ideas that have been marginalized owing to that lack of inclusion, the best course of action, according to Phillips, is to enhance the electoral opportunities of members of these groups within the political party structure.

Political Parties and Fair Representation

Parties become the relevant site of contention because they can aggregate interests in ways that groups based on identity cannot. One of the primary purposes of political parties is precisely to join citizens together who share some loose set of preferences and concerns in an effort to nominate and elect representatives to office who share those same (or some crucial part of that host) of interests. Thus if we want to get at what it is that citizens want, what better site for reform than political parties, which are designed specifically for this purpose? I find this emphasis on citizen concerns and preferences attractive. Although I defend the representation of "interests" and she employs "preferences" and "concerns," we are essentially talking about the same concept. Phillips simply shies away from using the term "interests" because of its tendency to denote disembodied choices. Regardless of this minor difference, I agree with Phillips that we ought to be concentrating on developing mechanisms that open the political agenda to previously neglected and ignored interests while remaining keenly aware of the fact that many of these marginalized interests are attached to the experiences of social difference.

The latter then justifies undertaking efforts that will increase the numbers of such groups within representative bodies.

It is her faith in the political parties as the site for cultivating fairer political representation, however, that I find problematic. Groups can certainly be represented, but those groupings are not likely to be based wholly or consistently on membership in a disadvantaged social group. Parties, on the other hand, are organized around shared views and interests. On Phillips's account, by going through the party organization to require party list quotas (gender) and targets (race and ethnicity), we can sidestep the problem of essentializing the interests of members of disadvantaged groups.

For Phillips, quotas are justified on the basis of political equality in that they do not freeze differences nor do they require members of a particular group to be the spokespersons for that group (and presumably only that group) (Phillips 1993, 98). Yet going through political parties to increase the numbers of members of marginalized groups and the interests they are likely to bring with them presents problems of its own. Political parties have historically reacted to calls for greater inclusion of female and minority candidates by running such candidates in races of lesser political importance or, even more likely, as "sacrificial lambs" in races that are practically unwinnable owing to the overwhelming support for the competitor (Andersen 1996, 111–40). Furthermore, parties are in the business of getting votes and, absent mechanisms for determining the interests of a majority of a given set of citizens (as opposed to those that are likely to vote), the party structure might not be the best location for increasing the representation of minority concerns. Simply requiring quotas and targets for disadvantaged groups on party lists neglects the process by which those candidates come to be there.

While parties are intended to be the site of mass participation and broad outreach to the overall electorate, it is clear that American parties are actually exacerbating inequalities. Instead of responsiveness to all or even most segments of the polity, US political parties cater disproportionately to those narrow segments of American society that have harnessed the most lucrative interest groups to do their bidding (APSA Taskforce Report on Inequality and American Democracy 2004, 657):

> [B]oth of the major political parties intensify the skewed participation in U.S. politics by targeting many of their resources on recruiting those who are already the most privileged and involved. Democrats and Republicans alike have become highly dependent on campaign contributors and activists and have become accustomed to competing for just over half of a shrinking universe of voters. What is more, political parties ignore parts of the

> electorate that have not turned out at high rates in past elections; the major parties have both become less likely to personally contact large numbers of less privileged and less active citizens—even though research tells us that personal contact is important in encouraging citizens to vote.

The problem is not only one of responsiveness but also one of outreach. Additionally, the fact that parties control the redistricting process (and in some cases it is now occurring more often than every 10 years), and do so with highly sophisticated technology that makes it possible to select voters that will send a candidate to state and national legislatures, renders parties less and less interested in listening and responding to, and acting on behalf of diverse interests.

Very recently, Mala Htun posed the question, "Is Gender Like Ethnicity?" when it comes to how nations attempt to include disadvantaged groups in legislative bodies (Htun 2004). Her response, after looking at 50 countries that allocate seats in national representative bodies by gender, ethnicity, or both, is a clear no. To increase gender parity, these countries overwhelmingly employ party list quotas; reserved seats are preferred by most of the countries seeking to enhance the representation of marginalized ethnic groups. So then the interesting question is why. Htun states,

> My explanation focuses on the varying ways that gender and ethnic identities intersect with partisan cleavages and on the distinct "work" performed by the different remedies for underrepresentation. Quotas, which make space within existing parties, are appropriate for groups whose boundaries crosscut partisan divisions. Reservations, which create incentives for the formation of group-specific parties and permit them direct representation, suit groups whose boundaries coincide with political cleavages. Since gender is crosscutting while ethnicity tends to be coinciding, women receive candidate quotas while ethnic groups get legislative reservations. Claims for inclusion via quotas pose less of a challenge to liberal institutions than claims to difference through legislative reservations. (Htun 2004, 439)

Ultimately, Htun wants to make a claim about the unique nature of certain kinds of groups and how the policies that we devise to address their needs should take into account how groups may differ from one another in important ways. "These distinctions are consequential for normative debates about social difference in a liberal polity. Gender- and ethnic-based demands present unique challenges to the liberal tradition. Because they are self-canceling, quotas produce the opposite effect on group difference than the self-reinforcing remedy of reservations" (Htun 2004, 451). By self-canceling Htun means that, once the group's claims are addressed, the group ceases to exist with respect to formal, legal recognition as well as coherence, since the unifying element that creates the group is the inequitable treatment received by virtue of being defined as different when no relevant differences actually exist; the elimination of those unfair policies and practices thus extinguishes any unity or distinctiveness that made the group a group. Thus gender quotas, according to Htun, are analogous to a *class action*, whereby the class exists only by virtue of some shared experience of a wrong that, when remedied, leaves behind no basis for group identification. The "difference" in this category is to be eliminated. Reserved seats for disadvantaged ethnic groups, on the other hand, is a self-reinforcing solution likened to a *group right*. In this case the remedy is one that seeks to "guarantee the continued existence of the group" (Htun 2004, 451). Here difference ought to be protected and empowered.

Htun's primary objective is to offer a compelling argument for why these 50 countries have a strong tendency to treat gender differently from ethnicity when it comes to allocation of legislative seats. Her conclusion, that these different approaches exist because gender cuts across partisan cleavages while ethnic identity tends to coincide with them, is plausible and compelling. It is the normative implications that are troubling. Not only is Htun arguing that we should be sensitive to the nature of the groups in question when devising schemes to enhance the representation of their interests, but she also implies that the general divergence in approach she describes is entirely appropriate. Although she briefly mentions that gender claims may occasionally be self-reinforcing just as ethnic claims can be self-canceling, she never explores just how often (or how infrequently) such claims might be (or are!) made. "Women seeking quotas," she explains, "aim to have their different position absorbed by universalistic institutions. Ethnic minorities demanding reservations want their particularism recognized and legitimized. These are opposing trajectories: women suffer from too much difference; ethnic groups from too little" (Htun 2004, 451). She concludes that adopting particular remedies will fundamentally shape the trajectories of a social group.

> A candidate quota promotes the integration of group members into existing political parties. Beneficiaries of the quota may later act to advance group interests, but they will do so—save at episodic moments—as individuals, not as a group. A legislative reservation produces the opposite effect: it strengthens ties among group members by connecting them through channels of representation distinct from those used for everyone else. (Htun 2004, 452)

Htun completes the argument with a warning that electoral engineers and scholars should beware of trading a "legislature of white men for a fragmented, even polarized political society" (Htun 2004, 452). Hardening difference is thus probably necessary for ethnic minorities; it is both unnecessary and rather dangerous to do so for women.

I bring Htun's study up at length because it raises the same deep difficulty that I see in Phillips's norm of convergence or androgynous ideal that we ought to be striving for and will be a marker of our success. Yet why suppose that most gender difference that makes a difference is the result of patriarchy? Might gender difference continue to exist in the absence of patriarchy? Even if we could determine that patriarchy created "gender difference" to maintain the gendered division of power, would that conclusion be meaningful given that there has been virtually no time in memory when patriarchy did not exist and thoroughly structure power in society? The bottom line is that the group difference that justifies gender quotas for Phillips (and presumably Htun) also justifies "group representation" institutionalized and formalized by making a public commitment to fund the organization and empowerment of historically marginalized social groups. In fact, the latter remedy does not presume that the group in question seeks the elimination or protection of difference. It is probably not always going to be clear cut for each group. Better this question be resolved by active and engaged self-identified members of the group than prescribed by an electoral and representational arrangement that resists such flexibility.

For Phillips's party list quotas to be meaningful in any truly representative sense, those candidates must arise from an engaged electorate in which all relevant interests are considered equally. That means that we must secure measures that aim to promote the political resources and influence of disadvantaged groups. There need to be incentives for citizens to do things differently and the provision of resources to make change possible. This will require electoral reform, in the manner described by Guinier in the previous chapter, that increases the likelihood of participation and political influence as well as public funding for the organization of marginalized groups, who often face higher participation costs and suffer greater economic burdens than the relatively privileged who tend to participate at higher rates.

Finally, quotas and targets may not secure an adequate number of members from any one group to provide meaningful representation. Iris Young (2000) makes a similar complaint when making the case against guaranteeing seats to members of historically marginalized groups based on proportionality in the polity). In the case of Native Americans, the example she employs, this might translate into a small handful of seats in the legislature, an insufficient number, in most cases, to make much of a difference in terms of policy outcomes.

Curiously, however, Phillips specifically rejects public funding of such groups. "But any call for funding or special status draws attention to the difficulties in establishing which groupings are relevant, and this lends weight to a more cautious approach. There is a powerful argument for enhancing procedures for group consultation, and for concentrating these on groups who have been disadvantaged in the current distribution of political influence. There is a much more shaky case for giving such groups definitive power" (Phillips 1993, 97).

The case may not be rock solid, as few things are, but it is no shakier than what she herself proposes. It is not at all clear that gender quotas escape the criticism of freezing differences. On the one hand candidate quotas would undoubtedly increase the number of women in elective office, and it is not unreasonable to conclude that more interests, ideas, and processes that benefit women would be some of the results of their increased presence. Furthermore, the case for gender parity in elective office is an easier case to make, given that there are (at least functionally) only two genders—rendering the question of which groups should count less complex and contentious. Nevertheless, women as a group are still being singled out for "special" consideration where quotas are concerned, and while it is explicitly not the intention for gender quotas to require that women be the representatives of their gender (Phillips actually sees quotas as being especially good at circumventing this), I am not at all sure that this will not be the outcome in practice—especially since there will presumably be no need to require or enforce quotas for men.

While Phillips wants to justify quotas on the basis of political equality rather than a notion of group representation, the outcome of such a requirement might in fact be far from equal. I am thinking here of the increasing precariousness of Affirmative Action in the United States, which does not even require quotas but is often argued to do just that. This is an argument that opponents endlessly trot out as a justification for its elimination. Although Phillips does not regard gender quotas in the name of parity as an instance of conferring special status, there is little doubt they will be greeted that way, particularly in America. Women will be widely regarded as having been singled out to receive special rights, and, once the women who benefit from this practice assume office, there will be an expectation on the part of many that they are there to represent their sex. The same expectations creep up over and over again of American women elected without the benefit of quotas.

With that said, I do not think quotas should necessarily be rejected based on these criticisms. My primary complaint is with Phillips's argument for quotas but against "funding or special status" on the basis that the latter freezes difference, pigeonholes the representative, and fails to sufficiently answer the question of which groups ought to count while the former virtually sidesteps all of these. All political representation is about the representation of some group and, to some degree, whatever proxy we use for the interests (be it geography, party, identity, or some other indicator), we run the risk of subverting intra-group disagreement and even freezing differences. For instance, imagine how class differences could be frozen within a system of geographic districting. It is not enough to argue that a particular approach to representation holds the capacity to freeze differences because, to varying degrees, they all do. Any phenomenon that, by its very definition, is for a part to stand for the (often heterogeneous) whole is almost assured to get it wrong on occasion. The challenge is for the part to represent the whole as faithfully and justly as can be made possible through fair and inclusive procedures and processes.

Even more importantly, Phillips blurs an important distinction between "enhancing procedures for group consultation, and for concentrating these on groups who have been disadvantaged" and "giving such groups definitive power" (1993, 97). The former she agrees with while rejecting the latter as dangerous for all the reasons stated above. Clearly for Phillips, the special funding of disadvantaged groups falls into the latter, and thus rejected, category of giving groups definitive power. This is a problematic position on two counts. First, given Phillips's strong defense of redistributive policies to begin to correct the political inequalities associated with historical deprivation—particularly the sexual division of labor—it is quite surprising to encounter a rejection of special funding for disadvantaged groups. Part of her rejection most assuredly stems from the dilemma of which groups would count for such funding, while a policy of redistribution would presumably entail a general transfer of resources from the "haves" to the "have nots." However, defining who the "haves" and "have nots" are still requires political judgment.

Second, I do not see that providing special funding for historically disadvantaged groups is granting them "definitive power." Definitive power in my mind conjures up earlier proposals by Iris Young (which she now rejects), for example, that would guarantee or designate seats in elective bodies to members of socially disadvantaged groups. Earmarking federal funds for distribution to historically disadvantaged groups to encourage political participation and organization *does not* bestow definitive power. Rather such public provision of resources begins to level the playing field and stands a good chance of fostering fairer opportunity to exercise definitive power. Ultimately, adopting a program to fund such groups confers no more definitive power than does instituting a policy of party list gender quotas.

Furthermore, a focus on *slates* of candidates rather than gender quotas or targets within the party structure is preferable for at least two reasons. First, an emphasis on slates allows for a diversity of interests and candidates to emerge from the disadvantaged group itself that is more likely to be representative of that group than party-selected candidates to fill targeted slots or quotas. In other words, a group's internal diversity, disagreements, and ongoing cleavages can be accommodated more effectively by amassing and running a slate of candidates that emerge from the group itself rather than candidates that are chosen by the party hierarchy that are more likely to be disjointed since they tend to be chosen based on possible district success.

Second, since the slates arise from the group members themselves, we can be more certain that the interests voiced and the candidates voicing them are the preferences of the group members and not simply preferences molded and conditioned by pre-existing party agendas. Parties *are* argued to be rather different organizational entities than groups separated out by social differences. Parties are organized around a general set of roughly consistent values while groups point to ascriptive characteristics about which no roughly consistent claims can be made. Of course such a clear delineation between these two types of groups is misleading. Members of the same political party often disagree about particular issues and even how to best understand fundamental party values. Evidence for this can be seen in the multiple manifestations of Republican and Democratic party members in the legislature (from moderate to conservative in the former to liberal to moderate in the latter). Whether we want them to or not, race, class, gender, and sexuality make a difference in American life. By granting such groups additional public funding to organize and participate more effectively, we need not assume a shared set of interests. We need only recognize that race, class, gender, and sexuality tend to structure people's lives in certain kinds of ways, particularly by limiting attractive educational, health, residential, and occupational opportunities. Recognition then demands that we implement new representational schemes that recognize, allow for, and encourage intra-group difference.

"Freezing differences" now seems to have taken over from the relentless cries of essentialism of a few years ago. They are, of course, two closely related criticisms, but they are not stand-alone claims that once lodged should serve as the death knell for a particular theory. We have to ask: in what ways does a given proposal freeze differences? Are there alternative approaches that could minimize this outcome? What might be the unintended consequences of adopting a particular scheme?

A Politics of Recognition *and* Redistribution

Potential political remedies such as proportional representation, party list quotas, and "targets" alone are not enough, however. Phillips argues that the turn toward politics to ascertain the proper approach to difference (or the focus on "recognition") has sidelined and even separated out concerns about economic equality (or a concentration on "redistribution") where "economic equality [is] understood not only as the equal right to participate in politics but as that deeper notion of equal intrinsic worth" (Phillips 1999, 15). Furthermore, "[t]he problem for democracy is not just how to equalize people's political resources but how to establish their equal human worth; the problem with economic inequality is not just that it constrains the exercise of political rights but that it shapes (and damages) perceptions of fellow citizens" (Phillips 1999, 83). Thus if we really care about recognition through difference, we must attend to the ways in which economic inequality informs and conditions how we view our fellow citizens, for

> even beyond the directly class inequalities, there are still strong links between economic circumstances and political equality. The association of certain categories of people with certain categories of work has particularly profound effects on a society's status order, and even the most rigorous campaign of cultural revaluation is unlikely to make enough difference to this. Some of the current inequalities between citizens do lend themselves to treatment via the cultural or symbolic order. All too many of them remain attached to economic location. (Phillips 1999, 98)

Thus a politics of recognition should not be in competition with a politics of redistribution. The former in fact requires the latter. For

> even if we tried to distinguish groups exposed principally to social inequality (homosexuals?) from those who suffer principally from economic inequality (the working class?), no group could be seen to occupy a truly polar position: they would all experience both. Phillips, moreover, 'would hazard a guess that any group that becomes a focus of resentment or object of disparagement will turn out to differ on some scale of economic comparison'. (Armstrong 2000, 368)

However, Armstrong cautions not to let this argument slip by unexamined:

> Could we think of any two groups (even, to be banal, supporters of different football teams) about whom this would not be the case? Would the fact that Wimbledon supporters are more widely disliked and poorer than Chelsea supporters generate a mandate for social reform? Almost certainly not, because the relationship between social and economic marginalisation has

> not been established, and it surely matters whether Wimbledon supporters are poor because of, or despite, their lack of favor. (Armstrong 2000, 368)

While Armstrong is right to raise the flag of caution when it comes to linking social and economic marginalization, his criticism in the case of Phillips is overstated. First, Phillips is not claiming that all members of a socially disadvantaged group will suffer economically as a result of that membership. Second, the example Armstrong employs neglects Phillips's characterization of relevant marginal groups. The differences that "matter" are those that inform, justify, and reinscribe political, social, and economic inequality. A better placed criticism would be one that hones in on unpacking what that pronouncement actually means, as it is clear from Phillips's writing that support for different football teams does not entail structured political and economic outcomes (see also King 1997 and Tilly 2001 for criticisms along similar lines).

Suzanne Dovi (2002) takes a slightly different tack and criticizes Phillips for her contention that

> the politics of presence should be treated as distinct from issues concerning class. Phillips offers several reasons for this distinction, e.g., the difficulty in defining class. However, Phillips admits that these reasons for treating class separately are 'insincere', stating that 'when it comes down to it, the real reason for my silence on class is simply that it does not lend itself to the same kind of solutions.' This admission implies that considerations of class cannot be adequately incorporated into the types of institutional reforms necessary for increasing the number of descriptive representatives. Interestingly, this admission contradicts her arguments for a politics of presence. (Dovi 2002, 739)

Dovi is correct to point out this particular flaw. I will argue later that Phillips uses this same problematic argument about class not lending itself to the kinds of institutional reforms as gender (quotas) to defend a certain silence on race as well. What seems particularly important to recognize in this regard is not so much that class disadvantage cannot be treated in the same ways institutionally as differences based on gender and possibly race and sexuality. Rather economic disadvantage is *one* quite potent indicator that, when joined with others such as health, education, and rates of incarceration, helps to identify which groups suffer from systemic inequality and deserve to benefit from measures that will increase their numbers in the representative bodies that make the decisions that affect their lives. I will have more to say on this topic in Chapter 5.

Just as there is a strong link between economic status and political equality, so too is there a link between identity and interests. Political equality thus requires, Phillips argues, an emphasis on both a politics of presence and a politics of ideas. Without the presence, in larger numbers, of the historically marginalized within representative bodies, we cannot meaningfully talk about a politics of ideas. While ideas and identities will never, of course, correspond in the same ways, we do know that our race, class, gender, sexuality, age, and class structure to a significant degree the way we live our lives (even what kind of life we are likely to live). Thus ideas, interests, and needs many times attach to certain groups of people with certain ways of life—ways of life that are crucially influenced by those ascribed characteristics.

We also know that, when there is an increase in the number of women and minority groups in representative bodies, they tend to propose (and pass) legislation and press issues that were previously ignored or never even conceived of as legitimate items for public, political consideration (Burrell 1994; Flammang 1997; Thomas 1994; Verba et al. 1993). Hence Phillips claims that we should require quotas for women but something like "targets" when it comes to ethnic minorities in an attempt to strike a balance between a politics of presence and a politics of ideas. Such a balance in the form of targets and gender quotas, she argues, should sidestep many of the problems associated with traditional conceptions of group representation: "The difficulties that bedevil group representation do not therefore affect the case for political quotas—or indeed for whatever alternative mechanisms could help establish political parity. The one point of overlap—and it is a difficult one—is in thinking about how far one should extend the principle of what I shall call 'mirror' rather than political representation: what exactly are the groups that should count?" (Phillips 1993, 99).

Yet as I argue above, quotas do suffer from some of the same difficulties as group representation (freezing difference, for example). Moreover, using quotas *within the party system* to increase the diversity of candidates is likely to accomplish little in terms of meaningful interest representation, especially in the absence of robust measures to foster the increased involvement of the members of the polity historically heard from the least. However, Phillips finally points to the key issue here: groups in fact do matter. If we agree that certain processes should be put into place that will foster greater parity, then which groups should be targeted? With this query, it appears that Phillips has grown much closer in thought to Young. She is convinced that there are measures to be taken to foment greater inclusion and fairer representation; we need only agree on some procedure for deciding what groups should be the beneficiaries of such measures. The union is an illusory one, however, for while deciding which groups should count (or establishing a process for deciding) is by no means a simple task, Phillips nevertheless quickly retreats.

Because there is no single fair way to make these judgments without rendering identity a one-size-fits-all garment (a cure worse than the disease), then we must remain satisfied, at least for the time being, with candidate quotas for women and "targets" for other groups. It is not at all clear, however, what these targets are and how they might be achieved. From the few indications she gives, the groups that Phillips has in mind are those on the margins owing to their race, ethnicity, or religion (or maybe some combination of these). How did she arrive at these groups and why is it that they can only be "targeted" in some vague non-institutionalized way while gender parity through quotas is to be written in institutional stone?

"My reservations," Phillips writes, "refer exclusively to that more ambitious step of institutionalizing group representation, for, in exploring the possible extension of feminist arguments into a case for formal and substantial group representation, I have come to the conclusion that the potential risks outweigh the gains" (Phillips 1993, 101). The risks primarily outweigh the gains because of Phillips's neglect of the differences that matter.

Conclusion

What Phillips is arguing for is, in fact, group representation, albeit group representation of a different sort. In fact, the fixed and narrow kind of group representation she speaks most often about and rejects would be dismissed by both Guinier and Young. Her neglect of the differences that truly matter leads directly to the rejection of a narrow and limiting kind of group representation. By not taking seriously enough the differences that make a difference in society, Phillips errs on the side of minimal intervention, a position much more consistent with a liberal understanding of equal treatment that demands the same treatment for all citizens with rare exceptions for extreme circumstances. Anything less will ultimately contribute to unequal (in the sense of unfair) treatment. However, this understanding of equality (which leads her to advocate a theory of convergence) certainly will not work well for particular cultures, races, or ethnicities that want their ways of life protected, and here Phillips has much less to offer. Phillips ultimately wants a non-essentialized form of group representation, a desire that is likely to go unfulfilled. I think that the claims about essentialism, however, are often overstated in the feminist literature. Iris Marion Young, discussed in the following chapter, can provide some insights into how essentialism or the freezing of differences might be limited.

Phillips is more comfortable with the case of gender because it has two fairly clear or recognizable categories. She claims that her rejection is not on the basis that it treats citizens differently and thus unequally but because "group representation" implies that there are identifiable interests associated with identifiable groups when we know that this is not always the case. Institutionalizing "group representation" thus has the unintended consequence of freezing differences—placing representatives of that group in the untenable position of passing along *the* group position—and thereby harming accountability and ensuring that deliberation and anything like a resolution would come to a standstill. Phillips rejects "group representation" because she regards it as the constricting formal or institutional recognition of some set of individuals who necessarily share something substantive (interests, beliefs, concerns, etc.) beyond a set of ascriptive characteristics. Such characteristics certainly imply no shared outlooks based on biology. However, even socially, Phillips implies that women, racial, ethnic, and sexual minorities do not share enough in terms of deprivation to justify or legitimize cordoning off such groups and according them special recognition.

This is mistaken. These social differences exist because they are the result of power structures erected to privilege (a "stacked deck," so to speak) in favor of the status quo or subjective norm. Instead we should think about these social groups as probably sharing many interests, outlooks, and concerns in the same way as those who share the same social class. We speak more easily about "class interests" (when we talk about them at all) than we do about gender or racial interests. Yet the latter are no more biological than the former.

However quotas for women, while they are not intended by Phillips to be for women as a group but rather for individuals who happen to be female and under-represented, could easily be said to foster the same unintended consequences. So why does she seek to guarantee gender quotas? Even if ethnic and racial minorities were more clearly delineated and we could agree on which groups should count, she would still have qualms about granting special representation rights to "groups" on the basis that "group representation" is only coherent insofar as it is premised on the notion that the group shares some set of interests. By freezing difference in this way, groups would be no better off, and may be even worse off, than without such recognition. However I will argue that we can and should engage in electoral reform *and* the public provision of resources to historically marginalized groups that will establish incentives for their increased political participation. The latter proposal is geared most directly at disadvantaged groups and is a form of "group representation." However that proposal does not make any assumptions about some single set of shared interests that can be neatly represented by a single member of that group (or some agreed upon spokesperson). All it does is recognize that some differences in society *do* make a difference and continue to effectively ignore the fact that difference does harm to democratic citizenship. Attempting to increase the participation levels of the historically marginalized need not mean that the group must speak in one voice. It is likely, however, that the voices will be conditioned by the experiences of difference, the same experiences that have pushed the members of those groups to the margins. If fair representation requires that all relevant voices be recognized, then measures to increase the participation of those from the margins is essential for determining what interests require representation.

Phillips emphasizes the importance of increasing the *presence* of members of historically disadvantaged groups in legislative bodies, which recognizes the worth, weight, and meaning of social difference for the life prospects of those members. She advocates party list gender quotas and racial and ethnic "targets" to increase their numbers while rejecting the move toward granting such groups "definitive power." Yet granting those groups public funds to organize and develop their own slates of candidates outside of a two-party system that has historically marginalized those same groups does not grant them definitive power. It does increase the likelihood that the presence of members and interests of marginalized groups will be increased to large enough numbers to produce real and relevant policy change.

However, it is not just being able to discern something like a definable group that should render it qualified for guaranteed representation. Particularly in the United States, this runs up against (legitimately or, more likely, not) questions of dessert: why should some groups be *guaranteed* a certain number of representational slots without necessarily having received the votes that would merit them? I think a case can be made about how fairness requires representational institutions to be reflective of the polity. Something fishy must be occurring if that body is consistently skewed demographically, particularly in the direction of white, middle- and upper-class males. Guaranteeing slots simply makes things fairer rather than less so. Even more problematic than that, however, is that such a practice implies a convergence between identity and interests, whether this is specifically disavowed or not. Such a policy is likely to normalize the connection so that racist, sexist and homophobic stereotypes are reinforced, and the deliberative environment that is supposed to entertain all relevant positions could very well devolve into assumptions and broadsides about "the women's bloc"—not simply because there is a discernable portion of females in the legislative body, but because that bloc was guaranteed. The guarantee, essentially, creates a built-in resentment factor. Shane Phelan, for example, writes about the importance of "getting specific" when it comes to the relationship between identity and interests. Getting specific "moves us from identity, with the assumptions of homogeneity and privatized consumerist concerns and agendas, to politics as an activity that is valuable in itself. The result is not the subsumption or transcendence of ‘identity politics’ but a recognition of the fullness of politics that cannot be encapsulated by identity” (Phelan 1994, 111). Indeed identity politics has had the tendency to devolve into a kind of interest group liberalism that portrays “masses of women, lesbians, and so on, with a unified interest” (Phelan 1994, 111). As more people within groups began to assert their “differences,” many feared the end of politics, for there would no longer be a mass foundation for mobilization and the generation of demands. However, “getting specific” is one way of intervening in this dialogue. By recognizing “specificities,” we acknowledge the important differences within groups without having to abandon the strength of a politics of identity that links us to allies and helps us diagnose injustice.

It might be better to simply require proportional representation of interests where presence will be increased by the public funding of historically disenfranchised groups. How would we decide which groups qualify? Not unlike the way in which Phillips comes to her conclusions about who should qualify for special representation rights: the groups will shift in response to the political and social context, but in many cases it will be based on an observable history of unjust treatment that continues to have a clear impact on life chances.

We can worry endlessly about intra-group difference and essentialism, but at the end of the day we know that some differences make a difference, and providing additional resources to those who share those differences in order that they might more effectively organize seems eminently wiser to me than engaging in minimal, strictly institutional reforms, the fruits of which are likely to be co-opted by the existing power structure. There are no definitives without context, and many of the questions surrounding who counts will have to be decided as a matter of politics, as Iris Marion Young attempts to explicate through an understanding of groups as structural phenomena that confer identifiable social perspectives that can and should be represented.

Chapter 4
Iris Marion Young and the Politics of Difference

> Relations of power are not in a position of exteriority with respect to other types of relationships (economic processes, knowledge relationships, sexual relations), but are immanent in the latter; they are the immediate effects of the divisions, inequalities, and disequilibriums which occur in the latter, and conversely they are the internal conditions of these differentiations. (Foucault 1990, 94)

> If inclusion in decision-making is a core of the democratic ideal, then, to the extent that such political exclusions exist, democratic societies do not live up to their promise. (Young 2000, 13)

Feminist identity theorists (many of whom do not deal explicitly with issues of political representation) focus upon conceptions of the self: what they mean for identity formation and how they inform the possibilities for real and emancipatory forms of human agency (Butler 1989, 1997; hooks 1992; Phelan 1989, 1994; Young 1990, 1997, 2000). Whether these feminist theorists are self-consciously interested in addressing the question of representation or not, they focus on some critical questions we ask ourselves as scholars of fair representation: who or what should we represent? If identities are constructed and thus contingent upon culture and experience, then should how we go about representing be contingent as well? How does the institutionalization of practices (such as representation) premised on certain understandings of who we are contribute to or hinder agency and the possibilities for democratic participation and citizenship?

Representation of Difference/Social Groups

> Systems of representation are most inclusive, furthermore, when they encourage the particular perspectives of relatively marginalized or disadvantaged social groups to receive specific expression. (Young 2000, 8)

Iris Marion Young has been a central figure in attempting to navigate issues of representation. She argues that there are identifiable groups that have been historically under-represented. Rather than insist on assimilation as a requirement for equal treatment, which would be patently inegalitarian, these groups should be granted special representation rights and a veto over policies that directly affect them and their ways of life. This politics of difference recognizes that "[g]roup-conscious policies are sometimes necessary in order to affirm the solidarity of groups, to allow them to affirm their group affinities without suffering disadvantages in the wider society" (Young 1990, 174; see also Kymlicka 1995).

The representation of social groups, Young maintains,

> [i]mplies institutional mechanisms and public resources supporting (1) self-organization of group members so that they achieve collective empowerment and a reflective understanding of their collective experience and interests in the context of the society; (2) group analysis and group generation of policy proposals in institutionalized contexts where decisionmakers are obliged to show that their deliberations have taken group perspectives into consideration; and (3) group veto power regarding specific policies that affect a group directly, such as reproductive rights policy for women, or land use policy for Indian reservations. (Young 1990, 184)

This form of representation, on her account, promotes better procedural and substantive justice. It provides better opportunities for agenda setting and increases the number and variety of voices heard. It enhances accountability, "because it serves as an antidote to self-deceiving self-interest masked as an impartial or general interest" (Young 1990, 185). Finally Young argues that her conception of representation "promotes just outcomes because it maximizes the social knowledge expressed in discussion, and thus furthers practical wisdom" (Young 1990, 186).

Young's is a much stronger conception of group representation than Guinier's or Phillips's in that it seeks specifically, formally, and quite directly to represent groups that have been marginalized on the basis of race, gender, ethnicity, class, sexuality, culture, and disability, to name a few. Group representation in the strong sense, however, is accompanied by problems of its own. What groups should qualify for such recognition? Will the representation of groups not have a balkanizing effect on the polity? What about disagreement within the group? How would the representation of groups accommodate cross-cutting memberships?

In an effort to answer some of these queries, Young, in her most recent work, *Inclusion and Democracy*, defends a conception of a structural group and an attendant group *perspective* (in contradistinction to opinions and interests) that she argues displaces criticisms of essentialism and intra-group conflict. Young argues that

> a structural social group is a collection of persons who are similarly positioned in interactive and institutional relations that condition their opportunities and life prospects. This conditioning occurs because of the way that actions and interactions conditioning that position in one situation reinforce the rules and resources available for other actions and interactions involving people in the structural positions. The unintended consequences of the confluence of many actions often produce and reinforce such opportunities and constraints, and these often make their mark on the physical conditions of future actions, as well as on the habits and expectations of actors. This mutually reinforcing process means that the positional relations and the way they condition individual lives are difficult to change. (Young 2000, 97–8)

Reminiscent of the work of Guinier and Torres on political race, Young is attempting to politicize identity, to draw our attention away from the ascriptive characteristics that mark difference to the ways in which possessing these characteristics structures one's life chances and outlook. It is not by virtue of the color of my skin or my gender that I am likely to feel an affinity with those who share those features. Rather it is because those characteristics have been given meanings that are readily observable in the form of social, political, and economic punishments and privileges. We can delineate groups based on their structural positions relative to those groups that tend to inhabit privileged locations.

If we can legitimately cordon off these groups because members of a given group share some over-arching outlook, then representation becomes an issue of fostering democratic dialogue, a dialogue that will only be meaningful, democratic, and fair if it fully recognizes all social perspectives. Thus

> [s]ocial perspective consists in a set of questions, kinds of experience, and assumptions with which reasoning begins, rather than the conclusion drawn. Critiques of essentialism rightly show that those said to belong to the same social group often have different and even conflicting interests and opinions. People who have similar perspective on social processes and issues—on the norms of heterosexual interaction, for example—nevertheless have different interests or opinions, because they reason differently from what they experience, or have different goals and projects … Social perspective is the point of view group members have on social processes because of their position in them. (Young 2000, 137)

The formulation of the group in terms of group experience rather than group "identity" is an effort to pull away from the biological and essentialist tendencies that haunt so much of the well-intentioned scholarship geared toward eliminating (or at least lessening) systems of oppression. Young is careful, however, to point out three important clarifications.

One is that structural groups should be differentiated from cultural groups.

> While they are often built upon and intersect with cultural differences, the social relations constituting gender, race, class, sexuality, and ability are best understood as structural. The social movements motivated by such group-based experiences are largely attempts to politicize and protest structural inequalities that they perceive unfairly privilege some social segments and oppress others. Analyzing structural difference and structural inequality, then, helps to show why these movements are not properly interpreted as 'identity politics.' (Young 2000, 92)

Instead of a politics centered upon identity, a categorization that has a tendency to essentialize ascriptive characteristics, a politics centered upon how the meanings we attach to gender, race, class, sexuality, and ability are likely to *structure* the social, political, and cultural opportunities unmasks *systems* of injustice that too often operate as though they are unbiased arbiters of merit.

The second issue related to this conception of social perspective is that it is something different than either interests or opinions. Certainly members of a structural group will disagree with one another when it comes to the interests they wish to pursue and the opinions they hold. A social perspective is a lens, developed as the result of experiences that are conditioned and structured by one's race, class, gender, ethnicity, sexuality, and ability (although these markers will vary on the basis of political and social culture). That lens is defined by a common outlook, point of view, or general philosophy about how the world works. African Americans, for example, are likely to possess a social perspective that identifies racism as a real and observable phenomenon. Yet black citizens disagree with one another with regard to how to go about eradicating racist practices and stereotypes, how engrained racist attitudes are, and how to prioritize eliminating racism, among a host of other competing concerns. So while we cannot and should not assume that members of a group share some specific set of interests or opinions that can then be represented in democratic bodies, Young maintains that we can rely on a shared group outlook.

Finally, there will probably be cases in which members of a structural group, typically because of cross-cutting memberships, will have more than one social perspective. In those cases, Young argues that perspective, and hence representation, be pluralized. This would mean more than one representative would speak on behalf of the group in a representative body such that each of the relevant perspectives is heard—not only in legislatures, but in other deliberative bodies, such as "courts, public hearings, appointed committees and commissions, and consultative processes" (Young 2000, 152).

In any case, representation should be thought of as a relationship. It is not only that citizens and representatives should establish long-term links, but citizens also ought to forge bonds with one another, as should representatives. "In a relational conceptualization, what makes a group a group is less some set of attributes its members share than the relations in which they stand to others. On this view, social difference may be stronger or weaker, it may be more or less salient, depending on the point of view of comparison" (Young 2000, 90). Yet when groups make political claims they "are not claims to the recognition of identity as such, but rather claims for fairness, equal opportunity, and political inclusion" (Young 2000, 107). By focusing on social perspective (and even plural perspectives) rather than ascriptive identity, members of groups are less likely to find themselves lumped among those with whom they feel little affinity and are not as apt to be singled out for unfair treatment based on biology and stereotypes (see Young 1997, 1993). "Perspective is an approach to looking at social events, which conditions but does not determine what one sees" (Young 2000, 139).

Indeed, difference or social perspective should be thought of as an asset rather than a hurdle to overcome in the quest for justice. Young argues that "group differentiation offers resources to a communicative democratic public that aims to do justice, because differently positioned people have different experience, history, and social knowledge derived from that positioning. I call this social *perspective*" (Young 2000, 136). Thus not only does greater inclusion serve as a condition for democratic legitimacy, but it also, she claims, increases the likelihood that the decisions that are made will be more just, as they result from a process in which our store of social knowledge benefits from all relevant perspectives.

Young has also amended her earlier thought on how to go about institutionalizing group representation. In *Justice and the Politics of Difference*, she argues for reserved seats in the legislature for under-represented groups but rejects a system of proportional representation. Proportional representation, she claims, can do both too much and too little. If it guarantees women 50 percent of the places in the legislature or other representative bodies, this might be more than what is necessary for women's perspectives to be heard and might make it more difficult for other marginalized groups to be represented. In addition, a system of proportional representation might lead to no seats for very small groups like Native Americans (Young 1990, 187–8).

Yet on further reflection and attention to scholars such as Guinier, Phillips, and Melissa Williams, Young rejects the reservation of seats for under-represented groups (at the very least they should be relied upon as a last resort)—acknowledging that such a practice comes with too many difficulties that require an essentialist posture at the stage of institutionalization. However, many of those issues can be resolved, she contends and I concur, by implementing a system of proportional representation within multi-member districts that employ cumulative voting or some other voting scheme that allows preferences to be ranked and encourages the production of candidate slates from the self-organized groups (groups that should be granted resources from the government to organize).

I am rather sympathetic to this idea of group perspective. Conceptually it carefully attends to the lived experiences of marginalized groups while clearly refusing essentializing categories. Young has often been criticized for essentialism (most recently by Tebble 2002), primarily from an ideological perspective that is hostile to the very notion of group representation. I think that this is a misinterpretation of her argument. However, I agree with Melissa Williams (1998) that we cannot neatly separate interests from perspective.

Young develops this idea of group perspective (as opposed to group interests), at least in part, to discourage a narrow partiality of vision. By representing group interests rather than group perspectives, we would fall prey to the same old liberal interest group dynamic that reserves no room for consideration of larger community goals. However, interests need not be so partial. Indeed, interests are a fundamentally social (i.e. group) concept. In fact, it seems to me that interests are what comprise perspective as she understands it.

Far from having "objective" interests that exist across space and time and supposedly reflect one's observable and unique circumstances, individuals tend to develop, alter, and jettison their interests based on changing experiences and circumstances. The experiences and circumstances that often have the greatest power with regard to issue formation are social class, race, ethnicity, gender, and sexuality. Interests cannot be separated from experience, and experience is tightly bound to patterns in how others perceive or recognize us. Social difference matters. That it matters is demonstrated repeatedly and visibly in measures of well-being like educational attainment, home ownership, physical and mental health, and employment. Thus interests are not just tied to experiences or circumstances that are mostly unique. Instead the experiences and circumstances most likely to affect and condition broad and more enduring interests are based on structures of power that habitually privilege some groups while marginalizing others. It is the experience of marginalization that renders interests its social or group character and justifies and even requires public recognition and remedy.

Members of marginalized groups will often share a set of interests that could comprise a perspective. However, there will be many occasions when there will be serious disagreement with respect to both interests and perspective. How would we even represent perspectives in a practical sense? Suzanne Dovi (2002) contends that

> the desire to avoid suppressing differences among members of historically disadvantaged groups can prevent theorists from articulating and defending reasons for preferring certain descriptive representatives over others. Simply to affirm all differences, as Young eventually does, ignores how certain politically salient differences between different groups in society (specifically between those who have been oppressed and those who have not) can justify the need for an institutionalized voice. Consider Young's example of the Asian American, who, she claims, has the perspective of an African American. This example shows how much she has weakened the claim that a historically disadvantaged group should be represented by members of that group. If one extends one's understanding of group membership so far as to include certain Asian Americans as members of the African-American community, then existing proposals for group representation, e.g., party list quotas, become untenable, for it is questionable whether such a person could contribute to the self-organization of an African-American community (or should count toward a party list quota for African Americans). If Asian Americans can possess an African-American perspective and thereby satisfy the requirements of being descriptive representatives for African Americans, so can whites. Young's revised understanding of representation could legitimate an all-male (or all white) legislature as adequately representing women (or people of color) provided they shared similar interests, opinions, and perspectives. The central claim of the literature on group representation—that historically disadvantaged groups need representatives from those groups—is seriously diluted by Young's notion of representation as a differentiated relationship. (Dovi 2002, 732)

In an effort to attend to both particularity and the larger goals of a democratic community, I agree with Guinier that what we have been doing and must continue to do is represent interests, albeit in a radically different manner than we do now. Yet Dovi places her finger on the problematic nature of going about this in Young's work.

Finally, because Young places marginalized social groups at the center of her analysis (not an altogether negative thing), she still wants to retain a group veto power over policies that directly and disproportionately affect marginalized social groups. Again, I am sympathetic to this proposal, especially with regard to Young's example of the use of Native American land. However this group veto right poses serious problems. It possesses a tendency toward conservatism (or maintenance of the status quo), removes certain items from the agenda that possibly should be up for democratic debate, and forecloses the kinds of democratic deliberation that Young so values.

Veto rights for disadvantaged groups have a propensity toward conservatism because, once legislation is proposed that centrally affects such a group and the group determines the effect to be adverse and vetoes it, the result is to maintain the present arrangement of things, which may or may not be ideal for any of the parties. In fact, knowing that moves in particular areas will always incur the group veto has the tendency over time, therefore, to remove such concerns from the agenda altogether. Veto rights also often serve as debate stoppers since the group can invoke them without discussing or negotiating with participants outside the group. If democratic deliberation is valuable, although often illusory when it can be initiated and maintained for any length of time, then any formal device that holds the power to stop discussion in its tracks (or stop it before it ever gets started) should be met with serious skepticism.

Brian Barry, for example, finds the entire multiculturalist approach to be dangerous and doomed to failure. He claims that

> In matters of common concern, it is hard to see why each person should not have an equal say in the outcome. Where a minority is constituted out of those who are on the losing side in a disagreement about the future of the institutions they share with the majority, there appears to be no case for building in special protections for the minority. It would surely be absurd to say that a minority defined in this way should have a veto on the policy favoured by a majority, or that its members should be able to demand that the policy with which they disagree should not apply to them. (Barry 2001, 300)

I want to be clear that my objection to Young's veto power is very different from that of Barry. He finds a minority group veto objectionable because he assumes the impartiality of present laws, practices, and institutions. If they are truly impartial, then a rule of strict equality and majority rule ought to satisfy the requirements of fairness on Barry's account. I, along with other feminist scholars, am unconvinced that our laws, practices, and institutions are anything like impartial. In fact, it is highly questionable if they could ever be so (and if that would be a good thing). This is precisely because the partiality that pervades public, political life has conditioned the rules that masquerade as impartial while producing vast social inequalities. Ideally, a minority veto might do wonders for protecting the ways of life of marginalized communities. Practically, however, such a veto power is likely to produce unintended consequences like dampened resolve to form coalitions, maintenance of the status quo, and the premature halting of deliberation.

When issues of this nature arise, the more prudent approach that diminishes these complaints would be to require a supermajority. On the upside, requiring supermajorities serves to protect minority interests. Proposed legislation to take over a portion of Native American land, for example, would demand that a significant number of representatives (anywhere between two-thirds and three-quarters of the membership) agree—not a likely outcome (at least far less likely than under a simple majority rule). In this way, minority and marginalized interests cannot be habitually thwarted.

Requiring supermajorities to enact decisions that centrally affect a disadvantaged group comes with its own set of potential problems, however. Chief among these is that a commitment to supermajorities has a tendency to operate in essentially the same ways as the minority veto and thus share the same serious problems. Because in reality a supermajority is virtually impossible to obtain, the complaint goes, historically disadvantaged groups possess the functional equivalent of a veto power.

While this criticism is a serious one, it is not devastating. First, while supermajorities are quite difficult to achieve, they are far from an impossibility, as evidenced by successful cloture votes in the US Senate. While far from easy or frequent, supermajorities are clearly possible. On this count, the difficulty in achieving a supermajority is a matter of degree rather than a definitive blow, especially given that each situation will be bounded by context, such as the issues at stake, the groups in play, how representative the legislative body is, and the overall political climate.

Second, it is not clear to me that the supermajority rule would have the tendency, particularly in the same strength, to significantly diminish deliberation or coalition-building. In fact, such a requirement seems to encourage and demand both for success. Third, there is something qualitatively and practically different about requiring a supermajority to pass and implement legislation that will directly (and often disproportionately and adversely) affect disadvantaged groups and bestowing a veto right upon those groups. In the latter case, the disadvantaged group can use the veto or threat of the veto to halt adverse legislation, but this can also result in serious obstructionism and maintenance of an unfair status quo. No matter how one interprets the outcome, however, if the disadvantaged group holds the veto power, it is much more likely to be labeled the "problem" in such scenarios. In the case of a supermajority, there would have to be significant coalition building and broad agreement within the deliberative body regarding the proposed legislation. Essentially, the onus would be on those who oppose the position of the historically under-represented. Those in opposition would have to persuade, cultivate, and bargain with their colleagues to amass the necessary support. Not only is this approach likely to result is more legitimate and acceptable outcomes, but it could possibly lead to better ones as well.

This does not mean that majority rule would no longer be acceptable. Procedures of majority rule and compromise are often "necessary and do not violate commitments to democratic legitimacy as long as persons and groups have reason to believe that they have had the opportunity to influence the outcome" (Young 2000, 118). Ultimately,

> [t]he representative is authorized to act, but his judgment is always in question. Whether he acted on authority is a question deferred to a later time, when he will be held accountable. The representative acts on his or her own, but in anticipation of having to give an account to those he or she represents. While there is no authorized mandate for many decisions, representation is stronger when it bears the traces of the discussion that led to authorization or in other ways persuasively justifies itself in a public accounting. (Young 2000, 131)

Reminiscent of Pitkin, Young clearly wants to establish the agency of the representative while binding her temporally and spatially to those for whom she acts. Yet she will be unable to act in a democratic fashion without input from the members of the polity. "Without such citizen participation, the connection between the representative and constituents is most liable to be broken, turning the representative into an elite ruler. For their part, representatives should respond to such participatory process" (Young 2000, 132–3).

Representation of Social Groups and the Necessity of Democratic Deliberation

The model of democratic process that Young endorses is one in which there exists a communicative orientation towards normative reason that fosters the transformation of private desire into public appeals for justice (Young 2000, 50). For too long, Young argues, there has been an unnecessary division between participatory and deliberative democrats over the question of political representation. Historically, participatory democrats have been dismissive of the very notion of representation, preferring instead to focus on direct involvement—particularly in more local, secondary institutions. By foregrounding and fortifying representation, participatory democrats are prone to claim, we have already given up on the democratic project.

Deliberative democrats, however, have insisted on the necessity of representation—arguing for it on practical grounds but also on the basis of its very legitimacy—so long as representatives maintain an ongoing and inclusive dialog with their constituents. "[R]epresentation is both necessary and desirable in modern politics. Rather than devaluing representation as such, participatory and radical democrats should evaluate the degree to which processes of authorization and accountability exist, are independent, and activate the constituency-inclusive participatory public opinion" (Young 2000, 133). Young points out that we should not see these two approaches as conflicting with one another. Representation need not, in and of itself, be undemocratic, but it certainly can be in the absence of political participation. Participation and representation must go together. However, it is important to note that the distinction she establishes between participatory and deliberative democrats is overdrawn insofar as there exists much more overlap between the two. Both in fact recognize the necessity and worth of cultivating strong norms of participation to strengthen the democratic value of political representation.

However, on what basis should a deliberative model of participation be endorsed? Young's move is not to defend deliberation as a first-order concern. Difference, or the structural group, holds the central location. This is because deliberation holds the greatest potential to provide for real inclusiveness and thus promote social justice. "I define social justice, then," Young states, "as the institutional conditions for promoting self-development and self-determination of a society's members" (Young 2000, 33).

Instead of treating difference as an obstacle, for Young it should be regarded as a resource. For only through the inclusion of all relevant social perspectives can we be sure, or at least more certain, that we have the social knowledge necessary to make prudent and fair decisions.

> A strong communicative democracy, I conclude, needs to draw on social group differentiation, especially the experience derived from structural differentiation, as a resource. A democratic process is inclusive not simply by formally including all potentially affected individuals in the same way, but by attending to the social relations that differently position people and condition their experiences, opportunities, and knowledge of the society. (Young 2000, 83)

With that said, Young wants to be clear that attaining consensus or arriving at the common good is not necessarily the goal of democratic deliberation. She writes, "While actually reaching consensus is thus not a requirement of deliberative reason, participants in discussion must be *aiming* to reach agreement to enter the discussion at all" (Young 2000, 24). Furthermore, one of the problems "with the assumption of a common good or shared understanding prior to or as a condition of political communication is that it obviates the need for the transformations from self-regarding to enlarged thought which … is an important aspect of a discussion-based model of democracy" (Young 2000, 42). However, an assumed common good can do far worse.

> The idea of a generalized and impartial public interest that transcends all difference and division makes it more difficult to expose how the perspective of the privileged dominates the public agenda than it is when people believe that politics is nothing but the naked competition of interest. Putting such a premium on a common good in the sense of values and interests we all agree we share, furthermore, is liable to narrow the possible agenda for deliberation and thereby effectively silence some points of view. (Young 2000, 43)

Theories of democratic process, and particularly pluralism in recent decades, continue to be plagued by this issue of agenda-setting. In the well-known debate among Manley, Dahl, and Lindblom, for example, the degree to which pluralism can account for itself when it comes to the nature of the items that officially appear for decision-making served as one of the central bones of contention (Manley 1983; Dahl and Lindblom 1983). The problems surrounding agenda-setting have by no means been solved. However, Young gestures to the ways in which actively requiring the representation of all perspectives in a political community makes it much more likely that historically privileged positions will no longer go unchallenged but will be recognized for their partiality. "A democratic public ought to be fully inclusive of all social groups because the plurality of perspectives they offer to the public helps to disclose the reality and objectivity of the world in which they dwell together" (Young 2000, 112).

However, "[n]ot only does the explicit inclusion of different social groups in democratic discussion and decision-making increase the likelihood of promoting justice because the interests of all are taken into account. It also increases that likelihood by increasing the store of social knowledge available to participants" (Young 2000, 83). This social knowledge in turn broadens our vision over time of what the possibilities really are in public life, how solidarities can be forged, and in what ways members of the community are helped and harmed by the decisions we make.

Although a great many scholars and political practitioners agree that a deliberative model of democracy is desirable, there remain a number of problems, especially with regard to its practicality as well as to what degree it can actually deliver on its promises of greater inclusion. Since a discussion-based democracy invites citizens to talk with one another about matters on which they disagree, there exists the very real danger that those citizens who are more skilled in public speaking and argument crafting (many of those, not coincidentally, who have benefited from good schools and economically advantaged neighborhoods) will have their concerns heard, while those not so skilled will continue to be drowned out or simply dismissed. A discursive democracy, the complaint goes, would be no different than our current form of representative democracy. The processes might be different, but the same old power relations would simply be grafted on to the new procedures.

Young takes this criticism seriously and supplements the careful work on fair deliberation by scholars like Gutmann and Thompson (1996), Benhabib (1996), Habermas (1985, 1), and Mansbridge (1983). She argues that a discussion-based democracy need not rule out certain forms of expression in favor of reasoned, logical, dispassionate argument. While those forms of communication are certainly acceptable, privileging them, Young acknowledges, does nothing to displace traditional power structures and cultivate a more inclusive forum.

Along with the more traditional forms of dialogue that valorize reason, as opposed to emotion, and structured, abstract argument, as opposed to personal stories, Young wants to make the case for the acceptance of *greeting*, *rhetoric*, and *situated knowledge* in deliberative fora. Greeting tends to be the starting point of any conversation, although it is often ignored by deliberative democrats as a simple custom that precedes the "real" activity of discussion, disagreement, and decision-making. However, greeting has the effect of recognizing others as participants in the matters at hand—as members who belong. Greetings, Young notes, may have to be renewed on occasion, but it is important that those greetings be aimed directly at the targeted groups. "One sign of the absence of such greeting is that a public debate across mass society refers to persons or social segments only in the third person, never addressing them in the second person. If a social segment rarely if ever appears as a group to whom deliberators appeal, … then that social segment has almost certainly been excluded from discussion" (Young 2000, 62).

If dispassionate, disembodied, and unsituated discourse has the capacity to exclude, then the acceptance of rhetoric and personal narratives could go a significant way toward limiting the exclusionary aspects of deliberative venues. The use of rhetoric, or symbols, emotion, and visual representations, allows users to convey not just substantive content but also places content in a particular context within which "the facts" obtain meaning.

The use of rhetoric, Young maintains, helps to get issues on the agenda, shapes claims appropriate to a particular public, and encourages the transformation from giving reasons to making judgments (also see the second chapter of Gutmann and Thompson 1996; Gutmann 1992, 1993). Rhetoric already drives what is often presumed to be dispassionate and objective recitation of facts. Facts have no meaning without context, and part of the argument Young makes is that we should unmask those claims and evaluations to reveal their partiality. However, the other, more important, part is that partiality is what we want. Given that she develops a case for regarding difference as a resource, it is a resource because of the perspectives it enlivens and includes that would otherwise remain dormant or disregarded as illegitimate.

Finally, situated knowledge or the relating of personal narratives has been a celebrated (and sometimes derided) activity in feminist theory and practice. Feminist standpoint theorists such as Nancy Hartsock (1995), Patricia Hill Collins (2000), and bell hooks (2000) contend that the inclusion of personal stories and perspectives—particularly those hailing from the margins—is necessary to do justice. It should be clear that Young heartily agrees with this argument. We also want to include the perspectives of minority social groups through their representatives in order to make legitimate decisions. Members of such groups should also be able to use the language of the personal in deliberative environments. Similar to the admission of rhetoric, accepting situated narratives as legitimate dialog in discursive venues allows citizens to place phenomena in a particular context, facilitates understanding (and often corrects pre-understandings), reveals the source of cultural values and practices, and increases social knowledge that aids in expanding thought.

Young's conception of democracy is often described as minimalist because she prescribes no single set of just ends that a democratic process should produce. However, her conception of deliberation is also minimalist in that it does not require the cultivation of special discursive skills, nor does deliberation necessitate that citizens be reasonable in the rather robust sense that many deliberative democrats have insisted upon.

> To be reasonable is to be willing to change our opinions or preferences because others persuade us that our initial opinions or preferences, as they are relevant to the collective problems under discussion, are incorrect or inappropriate. Being open thus also refers to a disposition to listen to others, treat them with respect, make an effort to understand them by asking questions, and not judge them too quickly. A reasonable respectful process of discussion exhibits deliberative uptake; when some speak, others acknowledge the expression in ways that continue the engagement. (Young 2000, 25)

Now, even by this standard, it could be objected that not many citizens would pass muster. As one reviewer of Young pointed out, "[i]f we do not expect to undergo transformation, we cannot be engaged in authentically democratic deliberation. By treating democracy minimally and procedurally as a means of collective problem-solving, Young does in fact achieve a balance between the real and the ideal that stands out brilliantly in the field of normative democratic theory" (Cruikshank 2002, 201). Calls for political transformation can almost always be labeled unrealistic given what we think we can expect from citizens operating under conditions of structural inequality. Yet Young takes these challenges seriously, as evidenced by her re-evaluation of what a reasonable citizen is and what should qualify as acceptable forms of democratic discussion.

> Because disadvantaged and excluded sectors cannot wait for the process to become fair, because there are often so many contending interests and issues, oppressed and disadvantaged groups have no alternative but to struggle for greater justice under conditions of inequality. The process of democratic struggle is an attempt to engage others in debate about social problems and proposed solutions, engage them in a project of explaining and justifying their positions. Disorderly, disruptive, annoying, or distracting means of communication are often necessary or effective elements in such efforts to engage others in debate over issues and outcomes. (Young 2000, 50)

Young's conception of rational citizen behavior is more expansive than that of so many previous scholars of discursive democracy—at least among those such as Habermas, Gutmann and Thompson, and Banhabib—who refer to the necessity of a more traditional understanding of careful reason-giving that then cordons off certain kinds of "unacceptable" speech.

Yet while Young argues for a more extensive realm of deliberative activity, her expectation that reasonable citizens are simply those that enter political debate with the expectation that their "opinions, their perspectives, and their interests will be transformed" is somewhat less than minimal (Cruikshank 2002, 201). However, the entire emphasis on the importance of citizens talking with one another about matters that affect them all is premised, at least to some degree, on the idea that there is some value to be gained from discussion, a value that would not exist if citizens did not possess the capacity to change their minds when presented with information they were previously unaware of or, better yet, information they were aware of but that has now been put into a context that sheds new meaning on old issues.

It is not that Young expects that all citizens, upon entering a deliberative forum, will be open-minded in the way she describes. However, there is good reason to believe that many citizens can be reasonable in this way and are better off, both in terms of democracy and justice, when they seek to justify their interests, opinions, and perspectives to those who will be affected by such decisions.

> If democratic communication is not simply deliberation among gentlemen who already share basic understandings, however, but is often a struggle among society's members to have their interests, experiences, and opinions recognized by others, and a struggle to persuade others of the justice of their claims, then a theory of communicative democracy should reflect on the normative meaning of all of the communicative interaction brought to such struggles. (Young 2000, 79–80)

Young's expansion of deliberation to include public acknowledgment, rhetoric, and narrative adds significantly to our ability to recognize and interrogate the normative meaning behind forms of argument and enhances the possibilities for a wider range of perspectives to be voiced and represented.

Conclusion

Brian Barry argues that

> the full implementation of the multiculturalist programme would be at best a mixed blessing even for its intended beneficiaries … My purpose has been simply to suggest that, *administered in doses of any strength you like*, multiculturalism poses as many problems as it solves. And, to return to my theme for the last time, it cannot in the nature of the case address the huge inequalities in opportunities and resources that disfigure—and increasingly dominate—societies such as those of Britain and the United States. (Barry 2001, 328; emphasis mine)

Special representation rights for groups, according to Barry, are anti-majoritarian and thus unfair. If citizens disagree, as they will, on what policies should be adopted based upon differing ideas about the ends of politics,

> we have a clear prima facie case for resolving disputes by adopting the policy favored by the majority. In matters of common concern, it is hard to see why each person should not have an equal say in the outcome. Where a minority is constituted out of those who are on the losing side in a disagreement about the future of the institutions they share with the majority, there appears to be no case for building in special protections for the minority. (Barry 2001, 300)

For Barry, the politics of difference in general, and Young's work in particular, rejects solidarity, fosters divisiveness, and it patently undemocratic (Barry 2001, 300).

However, others have been quick to point out that there is much fertile ground between the extremes of strict majority rule based on an individualist orthodoxy and a robust system of group representation. Elaine Spitz, for example, argues that

> [a]n individualist, one-man one-vote, standard overlooks the importance of discussion to majority rule's conflict-resolving function and underestimates social components of people's lives that need representation. Groups best express some aspects of political life because they involve a range of concerns whose significance is their shared quality—(e.g., class memberships or ethnic identification). These interests make sense only if pursued jointly with others. The group, therefore, more fully represents that interest than does any particular member. (Spitz 1984, 50)

So while I think this criticism from Barry is unconvincing, there is another more troubling claim made most recently by Barry, and Kukathas (1997) to some extent, that a robust defense of group rights may in fact prove more injurious to the members of those groups than a liberal individualist state ever could, insofar as a valorization of group autonomy neglects intra-group oppression by jettisoning a recourse to individual rights and pays insufficient heed to cross-cutting memberships simultaneously expressed (Crenshaw 1998; Weber 2001). Young begins with difference, and difference is fore-grounded in her exposition of just processes. In some respects Young's approach is Rawlsian, as she is attempting to do justice by improving the lot of the worst off. Although Young is certainly testing the limits of the liberal state as well as liberal civil society, her conception of the least privileged is more fully theorized than Rawls's.

For Young, justice can be approximated only by, first, theorizing from the bottom. While there are good reasons for beginning at that point, Young goes too far in the direction of strong or robust (i.e. fully institutionalized and rather restrictive) group rights and group representation. In *Justice and the Politics of Difference*, Young argues for reserved seats for social groups, a practice she now rejects for state and national legislative bodies, for example (but not necessarily for smaller, local representative bodies). She now rejects this move at the state and national levels precisely because of the problems rehearsed here that such guarantees entail.

The claim I want to make is that Young places structural difference at the center of her analysis and, in so doing, can only partially realize her goals for greater and more meaningful inclusion. So long as group representation is institutionalized, even on the basis of structural groups with plural (but identifiable) social perspectives rather than on strict identity, the fluidity of identity is undermined and the tendency to freeze differences and quell dialogue both within and without groups increases.

Mark Warren also recognizes the centrality of difference in Young's work and writes "it is important to Young's take on deliberative democracy that she put inclusion in the foreground rather than deliberation," for "if we hold that democracy is, in the first instance, about including all potentially affected by a decision, then we are less likely to confuse other ideals with democracy … [I]f inclusion takes priority, then deliberation follows, simply because inclusion means decision makers are less able to make decisions using nondiscursive means" (Warren 2002, 648).

However, it is not only that Young foregrounds difference in order to make the case for discursive decision-making. She starts with a commitment to the reality and meaningfulness of groups and then seeks to accommodate that commitment by conceiving a non-essentialist way to define group membership so that (group) representation rights can be assigned. This approach, which I find superior to previous work in favor of group representation rights, nonetheless compromises her ability to fully recognize the persistence of two related problems.

First, while recognizing the social perspectives of structural groups avoids some of the pitfalls associated with the recognition of difference on the basis of simple identity, it continues to stifle intra-group difference. Although Young argues that there will be cases in which the social perspective of these structural groups will necessarily be plural, I think it is clear that institutionalizing and normalizing the connection between the structural group and an associated social perspective (even *perspectives*) will have the tendency to stifle new and innovative ways of thinking about and responding to old questions. This tendency is an outgrowth of a too strong interpretation of social perspective, something Young attempts to guard against by differentiating perspective from interests and opinions.

Thus as women, we are certain to disagree with regard to our interest in and opinions about whether new mothers should return to full-time employment. However, we are likely to share a perspective that women in the aggregate are unfairly burdened by virtue of their gender. If we take Young at her word, then social perspective appears too weak; it is a rather blunt tool for getting past ideas and beliefs and on to policy proposals. Rather than valorizing the social perspectives that hail from the experience of difference, it is more prudent to leave what comes from a given structural group under-theorized or open-ended—as a matter to be discussed, pluralized, and revised as deemed necessary by those who consider themselves members of the group.

Second, Young wants to retain veto rights for groups in matters that disproportionately affect them (one example from *Justice and the Politics of Difference* is that women ought to have a veto over measures that would limit their reproductive freedom), a move that is likely to limit (and even halt) discussion among groups—something Young clearly wants to avoid—and sets the stage for further oppression and "ghettoization" of the group that possesses and employs the veto. Thus the first criticism limits discussion and democratic reach *within* the group, while the second diminishes the same *among* groups.

Nevertheless, I find Young particularly strong and useful on two fronts. The first is her more expansive and, to some degree, less onerous vision of deliberative democracy. While virtually any call for more robust citizen participation can be brushed aside as overly demanding and even utopian, Young has advanced the debate beyond the requirement of some set of previously agreed upon principles, values, and standards.

> Whether the principle of constituency is geography, residence, belief, financial interest, organizational or occupational interest, or social group position, members of the constituency are better represented when they organize together to discuss their agreements and differences with each other and with officials. In the first place, any constituency is internally differentiated and has to be organized in relation to a representative. Individuals are better represented, furthermore, when representative bodies are plural, and when individuals have plural relationships to representatives, in both political and civic organizations. (Young 2000, 143)

There are no requirements for face-to-face interaction, nor are there demands that claims be fashioned along rigorously logical, dispassionate, or deductive lines.

The second is Young's idea of structural groups with social perspective(s), which to some degree escapes the essentializing features of thinking of groups more narrowly in terms of some shared identity. Turning the discussion away from ascriptive characteristics and the associated tendency to then foreground biology to the ways in which race, class, gender, sexuality, ethnicity, and ability *structure* the lives individuals are likely to experience goes a long way toward shoring up a sense of agency while breaking down negative and essentializing stereotypes.

An emphasis on *structural* groups draws our attention to the norm of inclusion that otherwise remains exclusionary as it masquerades as a universal and objective norm. Young argues,

> [i]nclusion increases the chances that those who make proposals will transform their positions from an initial self-regarding stance to a more objective appeal to justice, because they must listen to others with differing positions to whom they are also answerable. Even if they disagree with an outcome, political actors must accept the legitimacy of a decision if it was arrived at through an inclusive process of public discussion. The norm of inclusion is therefore also a powerful means for criticizing the legitimacy of nominally democratic processes and decisions. (Young 2000, 52)

A norm of inclusion, by which she simply means active and vigilant efforts to consider relevant perspectives, need not *require* the presence of all structural groups in deliberative bodies, for the attendant problems I outlined above. What a norm of inclusion and an emphasis on structure does, however, is establish a basis upon which to decide what constitutes a group and which groups ought to count for additional scrutiny.

It is on this basis that those marginal structural groups can and ought to be singled out to receive public funding, rather than guaranteed admittance on lower-level discursive fora, for the purposes of fostering solidarity, grassroots organization, and the selection of candidates that represent the perspectives of the self-identified membership. Young seemingly agrees as

> people collectively exercise positive power through civil society in a variety of ways. People acting in civil society to develop new ideas, disseminate alternative practices, or organize public criticism of state economic power, form solidarities for both the privileged and the relatively disadvantaged. They invite members of the society to discuss problems either in order to change state or corporate policy, or to foster change in society directly. All these activities refer to the value of self-determination, the primary aspect of social justice that associative activity outside state and economy promotes. To the extent that associative activity enables public expression of particular ways of life or provides goods and services, it also contributes to promoting the value of self-development. Thus those who argue that diverse and broad civic associational life is a crucial basis for democracy have good grounds for their claims. (Young 2000, 179–80).

Nevertheless, to approximate what Young details above, she need not institutionalize group representation (especially the group veto) so strictly and aggressively. Such institutionalization is likely not only to freeze differences and diminish possibilities for widespread democratic dialog, but also tends to limit the likelihood of forging cross-group alliances and political solidarity. This does not mean, as Barry argues, that a multiculturalist program "administered in doses of any strength you like" will pose as many problems as it solves (2002, 328). Ignoring difference altogether or making difference the central concern for justice is likely to maintain an unfair status quo or reinforce the very problems an emphasis on difference seeks to ameliorate, respectively. Ultimately this either/or proposition is a false dichotomy. It is precisely in the strength of the dose that a potentially robust solution resides, not in jettisoning group considerations altogether.

Chapter 5
Representation and the Politics of Democratic Inclusion

> I am located in the margin. I make a definite distinction between marginality which is imposed by oppressive structures and that marginality one chooses as site of resistance—as location of radical openness and possibility. This site of resistance is continually formed in that segregated culture of opposition that is our critical response to domination. We come to this space through suffering and pain, through struggle. We know struggle to be that which pleasures, delights, and fulfills desire. We are transformed, individually, collectively, as we make radical creative space which affirms and sustains our subjectivity, which gives us a new location from which to articulate our sense of the world. (hooks 1990, 153)

The representation of interests is the best way to recognize particularity. Indeed we always seem to be attempting to represent interests while never being able to fully get at them. Instead we attempt to find and adopt acceptable proxies for interests. As we have seen, geography poses serious problems for ascertaining and organizing interests. It also mires us in districting disputes that seem to have no acceptable resolution. Even Iris Marion Young's social perspective held by a structural group is a proxy for interests. So long as the representation of social perspective (even pluralized perspectives for a given group) mutes intra-group difference, social perspective may not be that much more effective than geography or identity for getting at what most matters politically to the members of a polity.

Electoral Change and Party Politics

We can represent interests more directly by altering our voting scheme, and there is solid evidence not only that new schemes offer attractive and plausible options, but also that there are good reasons to be assured that they will lead to more descriptively and substantively representative bodies.

> Both cumulative voting and limited voting systems have been adopted in response to lawsuits, or the threat of lawsuits, alleging minority vote dilution. Courts have approved the adoption of these systems when they provided the basis for the settlement of such suits, and the Department of Justice has almost invariably granted preclearance to them. Cumulative voting has

> been adopted by almost sixty counties, municipalities, and school boards in five states, while limited voting has been adopted by almost forty such units, also in five states. Elections have now been held under these voting rules in almost all of these settings. These elections have demonstrated that when the minority's percentage of the electorate has exceeded, or even approached, the value of the threshold of exclusion for one of these systems, minority candidates have almost always been elected. Exit polls conducted at a number of these elections have further confirmed that these minority candidates, many of whom were the first minority person ever to be elected to the particular governing body, have been the choices of minority voters. These results have been found regardless of whether the relevant minority has been African-Americans, Latinos, or Native Americans. (Rush and Engstrom 2001, 44)

(See Engstrom and Barrilleaux 1991; Engstrom, Kirksey, and Still 1997; Engstrom, Taebel, and Cole 1989; Hodgkiss 1999; and Mulroy 1995 for the specific results and methodology of these studies.)

> Thus alternative voting schemes have not only been adopted, embraced, and proved (at least from the evidence thus far) successful in various states and municipalities, but they have also been accepted by the courts as legitimate and even necessary measures to improve the legitimacy and responsiveness of representative bodies. (Amy 1993)

The Illinois state legislature used cumulative voting from 1870 to 1980, and it has been used to resolve voting rights cases for city council elections in Amarillo, TX and Peoria, IL, for county commission elections in Chilton County, AL, and for school board elections in Sisseton, SD, in addition to more than 50 other jurisdictions. In Maryland in 1994, a federal judge imposed the implementation of cumulative voting to resolve a voting rights case filed by the American Civil Liberties Union. Federal Judge Joseph H. Young struck down Worcester county's at-large designated-post election system for violating the Voting Rights Act, stating that the system "interacts with past and present discrimination to deprive African Americans of … the same opportunity as other members of the electorate to participate in the political process and to elect representatives of their choice" (Jeon 1999, 1). The Fourth Circuit Court of Appeals later affirmed the district court's finding that the at-large system violates the Voting Rights Act.

> The Court forcefully rejected the County's reading of *Shaw v. Reno*, noting that *Shaw* had found use of race in the redistricting process objectionable only in those exceptional cases where 'traditional districting principles are ignored and the resulting districts are so geographically bizarre that they are explainable only as an act of racial segregation.' The Worcester case did not present this problem, the Court held. Setting an important precedent, the

> appellate court also rejected the County's contention that cumulative voting is a 'radical departure' from traditional election practices, or one that may not be judicially imposed to remedy a Voting Rights Act violation. Quoting the concurring opinion of Justice Clarence Thomas in *Hall v. Holder* (which, in turn, had cited Judge Young's decision in the Worcester case) the Court wrote 'nothing in our present understanding of the Voting Rights Act places a principled limit on the authority of federal courts that would prevent them from instituting a system of cumulative voting as a remedy under Section 2.' (Jeon 1999, 2–3)

Even more recently, Port Chester, NY has adopted cumulative voting to elect representatives to the village's Board of Trustees. Latinos make up 49 percent of the village's population of approximately 28,000 people and, prior to the new electoral scheme, no Latino had ever been elected. In fact, the "odds against winning have been so daunting, Latino advocates say, that only two Hispanic candidates have ever been on the ballot, most recently Cesar Ruiz, who won nearly the entire Latino vote in 2001 but still lost the election" (Semple 2010). Following the implementation of this new electoral arrangement in 2010, Port Chester elected its first Hispanic member of the Board, Luis Marino.

Also in the state of New York, there is currently a push to institute what supporters call "instant run-off voting." While this voting system would not solve the problems posed by a reliance on single-member districts, it would allow voters to rank-order candidates. In the event that a race is close, the votes can be re-tabulated to reflect secondary and even tertiary preferences without the need to hold a run-off election, which tends to draw significantly fewer voters than the original election.

However, why is cumulative voting preferable to limited voting or preference voting? Limited voting would make the simplest change to our present system. Under a system of limited voting, a voter is allowed, in a multi-seat election, a number of votes less than the number of empty seats. Voters are permitted to cast only one vote for any single candidate, and winners are determined by a simple plurality rule. "Limited voting provides minority voters with an opportunity to elect candidates in the multi-seat context by reducing the ability of a cohesive plurality to win every seat. The restriction on the number of votes reduces the larger group's ability to submerge the votes of a smaller group" (Rush and Engstrom 2001, 37).

Another possibility would be a shift toward preference voting (also referred to as choice voting or the single transferable vote). Under this system, each voter is allowed to cast only one vote for any particular candidate, similar to limited voting, but the voter also has the opportunity to rank-order the candidates.

Votes are less likely to be wasted under such a system (either cast for a losing candidate or counted as a surplus for a candidate who would have won without it). Preference voting is said to increase the likelihood that citizens will cast a vote for a winning candidate. "The winning candidates in a preference-voting election are those whose votes equal or exceed a specified number. This number is usually based on the *Droop* quota, which is the lowest number of votes that can be required for election and yet limit the number of seats to be filled" (Rush and Engstrom 2001, 39). The droop quota is simply a threshold for determining a cutoff for the number of seats to be filled and the candidates who are potentially eligible to fill them based on the percentage of #1, #2, etc. rankings garnered.

While either of these alternatives might be acceptable, cumulative voting provides citizens with the same number of votes as there are seats available. The voter can then parcel out those votes on whatever basis she finds appropriate (on the basis of a shared ideology, local or geographic concerns, identity, particular policy positions, etc.). All votes can be cast for the preferred candidate, used to indicate a descending order preference, or parceled out equally among some group of candidates (who maybe all share some set of commitments that are important to the voter). The vote, under a cumulative voting scheme, becomes more like one of those multi-use household tools that can operate as a screwdriver, stud finder, or flashlight, depending on what you require at a given time. Those votes become proxies for whatever the citizens casting them deem important. If a citizen wants to concentrate votes on a candidate based upon the candidate's race, he can do so. If he finds the candidate's party affiliation, positions on crime, or occupation more salient, he can cast his votes accordingly. Such an electoral system would allow the citizens to group themselves rather than establishing some preconceived basis for distinction.

Thus cumulative voting would require a movement toward multi-member districts, but it could maintain two aspects of representation that Americans tend to hold onto rather tightly: geography and candidate-centered elections. Melissa Williams argues that

> it would be desirable to maintain some geographic basis of constituency definition, both as a matter of cultural continuity with the tradition of geographic representation (a Burkean gesture) and because of the importance to many citizens of constituent service as a form of political representation. Finally, maintaining some geographic basis of representation is important for the purpose of maintaining clear and close communication between representatives and constituents, and for constituting 'town hall' meetings and focus groups within constituencies. (Williams 1998, 234)

Furthermore, cumulative voting, as well as limited and preference voting, are often referred to as semi-proportional representation (PR) electoral systems in that these voting schemes retain what are often regarded as the greater strengths of proportional representation (increased participation given the heightened likelihood of casting a vote for a winning candidate and more meaningful representation of minority interests that would otherwise tend to be ignored by the single winning candidate from a given district) without requiring voting based upon party lists.

While Mark Rush is critical of approaches that specifically seek to equalize representational opportunities for historically marginalized groups, he does recognize the potential for something like cumulative voting (or some other semi-PR scheme) to extricate us from the controversy between a United States that is committed to single-member districts and the fact of geographically dispersed interests.

> Alternative electoral systems offer a way out … because they would allow for (without guaranteeing) political results that would accommodate minority representational opportunities. Generally speaking, the alternative electoral arrangements advocated by reformers such as Dick Engstrom are *candidate centered*. That is, they allow voters to pick and choose among individual candidates without being forced to choose among party lists. In this respect, alternative systems such as cumulative voting and the single transferable vote cut a path midway between the American SMP [single member plurality] system and full-blown European PR systems. Accordingly, their impact might not be as drastic as a conversion to PR. (Rush and Engstrom 2001, 119)

So long as US voters remain more attached to particular candidates than party ideologies, the benefit of a semi-PR system is clear; citizens can continue to vote for candidates rather than a party label, and the shift to the new voting system need not be so disruptive and confusing.

However Thomas Christiano, for example, maintains that party list proportional representation is actually superior. On his account, parties ought to be the primary players for four reasons. When individual candidates are the focus of partisan politics, (1) attention tends to turn to matters of personality, which detracts from matters of substance, (2) the choice among candidates becomes more obscure and requires citizens to have more information in order to make decisions, (3) fragmentation increases as each candidate is out for him or herself, and (4) matters of competence become of real concern, as candidates "vary a lot in their abilities to negotiate and compromise" (Christiano 1996, 223; see also Christiano 1990).

Lisa Disch has also recently argued in favor of a more party-centered approach, based on the "fusion" concept, to increase the representation of historically marginalized interests and decrease the problem of wasted votes.

> Also known as 'cross-endorsement' or 'multiple-party nomination,' fusion is a nominating strategy third political parties commonly used in the nineteenth-century to sustain themselves within the winner-take-all system. In a fusion candidacy two or more parties combined forces to run a single candidate on multiple party lines in the general election. Fusion is not an endorsement. It is a multiple-party nomination in which typically a dominant-party candidate ran on the lines of an established party and a third party. The votes were first tallied separately so that each party to the alliance had a precise accounting of its contribution to the outcome, then they were added together to determine the candidate's total share of the balloting. (Disch 2002, 12; candidates and parties employ this tactic in New York State)

Disch's primary point of intervention and justification for this alternative approach is based upon the tyranny of the so-called US two-party system. She argues that

> The tyranny of the two-party system is this: that a regulatory system born of politics comes to be taken as a defining feature of American political identity, that an ultimatum—vote for one party or the other—stands as the epitome of democratic choice. Would it 'collapse in an instant if the tubes were pulled and the IV's were cut?' Probably not. Although electoral duopoly *is* a regulatory system, it is not *merely* one. It is also a common sense that persuades most of the United States electorate to either vote within its terms or not vote at all. This is the most tyrannical aspect. It resigns us to the choice between the two dominant parties, and even threatens to punish us if we refuse that choice (our vote will either be 'wasted' or 'spoil' the election for the dominant-party candidate we would otherwise prefer). (Dsich 2002, 127)

Disch thus deftly illustrates the ways in which two-party competition is not the last word in institutionalizing democratic representation. Two-partyism has often been considered definitive in this sense for its power to produce majoritarianism. This majoritarianism, however, as Disch and others point out, is false or manufactured—especially when it comes to the role of the Electoral College in presidential contests. Following the 2000 presidential election, many citizens and public figures claimed that the narrowness by which that race was won demonstrated the importance of voting and making every vote count. Yet the Electoral College, which is the national representation of geographic regions, either magnifies the margin of victory (producing a majority where no majority exists) or distorts the outcome altogether (granting victory to a candidate who did not even garner a plurality).

While these are serious concerns, I am not at all sure that making parties the central players (as Phillips, Christiano, and Disch prefer) puts us in any better position to claim that we can more effectively represent interests. It is a possibility that a politics centered around parties would diminish the emphasis on candidate personality. It is not likely to eliminate it, however, as the politics of personality remains in countries that employ party list PR. This criticism further implies that citizens cannot or care not to distinguish between personality and substance. On the one hand, the former can legitimately become an issue of the latter. Matters of personality are not always "distractions." On the other hand, it should be up to citizens to decide what counts as substance.

Although candidate-centered elections may require citizens to gather more information in order to cast an informed vote than in a system premised on the party, a reliance on party label and broad ideology might have the tendency to obscure the specifics of policy positions and agenda items. In addition, the concern with fragmentation in legislative bodies may be overstated, at least in the American context, which is widely regarded as the most fragmented of democratic party systems. While there are no formal or institutional sanctions available in the US legislature to compel party discipline, the parties have, since a re-organization in the mid-1970s, emerged as revived bodies. The party caucus is now in a more centrally powerful position. It decides on leadership, committee assignments (no longer simply on the basis of seniority), and a general direction for the party (of which the whips remind the members; see Eldersveld and Walton 2000, particularly Chapter 6, for a more complete explication of the "revived and relevant" US parties). Finally, insofar as American parties remain central in the recruitment of candidates for national office, this concern about varying levels of competence in a candidate-centered system is virtually irrelevant.

In addition, moving immediately to a stricter PR system would be problematic in the American context, as we have fewer institutional measures (sanctions) to encourage party discipline. Thus the bonds between representative and constituent might be more tenuous if citizens vote for a party, the members of which may not share the same perspective on how to best realize rather vague party goals and operate in an institutional context that cannot require (and often finds it difficult to pressure) member agreement and compliance.

Another potential problem of semi-proportional systems is that they are likely to attract

> more minority candidates to a contest, inevitably inviting dispersal of minority votes over too many candidates. As a result, minority candidates may defeat each other. Indeed, majority representation may be limited if too few majority candidates run. To produce reliable results from limited or cumulative election systems, parties or groups seeking representation must attempt to exercise control over the number of candidates that enter a given race, and individual voters must understand how to vote strategically. Minorities that may or may not be residentially segregated but that learn to limit nominations and vote cohesively can gain representation in at-large LV [limited voting] or CV [cumulative voting] voting systems. (Barber 2000, 71)

Thus "[t]he principal disadvantage of LV and CV is that in the absence of well-organized nominating and voting, minority candidates may lose because their support is either diffused among too many candidates or wasted in surplus votes" (Barber 2000, 79). This potentiality should be mitigated, however, by the federal funding of historically disadvantaged groups in order to organize and run slates of candidates that they can limit strategically.

Finally, a semi-PR system based on cumulative voting would not solve the very important and enduring problems associated with how to draw district lines fairly. Nevertheless, it is not that geography itself is so terribly problematic as a proxy for interests (though to be clear, it *is* problematic). The issue is rather the establishment of districts from which only one representative can be elected. Pluralizing representation within geographic districts will not eliminate the problem of *how* to draw those districts, but it will lessen the stakes associated with gerrymandering and redistricting. For ultimately, "the only principle compatible with a principle of political equality in this context is a principle of voluntary proportionality between the number of citizens who support each of the different overall aims and the number of legislators committed to those aims in the legislature" (Christiano 1996, 220). Yet we clearly do not have a system that works toward that end. Instead we engage in high-stakes legal and political quarrels about how to fairly draw district lines from which only one representative will emerge.

There has been further criticism lodged against alternative voting schemes aimed to increase inclusivity by both scholars and, to a much larger degree, by popular political culture. That criticism is voiced clearly by Mark Rush, who claims,

> [c]ritics of the VRA [Voting Rights Act] and the Supreme Court decisions that have advanced the cause of minority voting rights contend that *any* racially motivated attempt (even a benign one) to tinker with the electoral system violates the Fourteenth Amendment's guarantee of equal protection.

> They have a point. If it is constitutionally repugnant to gerrymander minority groups out of power, how can it be acceptable to gerrymander them into power? One person's benign attempt to help a historically disadvantaged racial group is another's racially motivated attempt to condition electoral outcomes. (Rush and Engstrom 2001, 116–17)

This criticism has widespread appeal but is fundamentally misguided. First, there is substantial rhetorical appeal to the kinds of statements that allege that targeting under-represented groups amounts to reverse discrimination (it has had significant purchase in the debates over Affirmative Action and federal hate crimes legislation, for example). However, such charges can only make sense if we understand the pursuit of power to be a zero-sum enterprise; by attempting to lessen and even eliminate political, social and economic barriers for women and minority groups we necessarily take a correlative amount of power and influence from the privileged. Yet we know that power does not necessarily operate in this way. Some power will undoubtedly have to be relinquished by the privileged for the sake of greater inclusivity, but it is not as if there is some finite cache of power, a withdrawal from which depletes the store by roughly that amount.

Second, the power possessed by those who are relatively privileged by their race, class, gender, ethnicity, sexuality, and/or ability comes at the expense of the less privileged. Agitation to improve the chances of electing more women and minorities *is* an attempt to "condition electoral outcomes," but not in the way that Rush characterizes it. Instead, they are attempts to *condition fairer outcomes* from concepts, practices, and institutions that already privilege white, middle- and upper-class, heterosexual men.

Beyond these electoral reforms, rectifying the participation imbalance will require, at a minimum, complete public funding of political campaigns, on the one hand, as well as public funding of disadvantaged groups for mobilization and development of candidate slates, since "[i]n order to exercise the fundamental rights to which citizens in a democracy are entitled—to vote, speak, publish, protest, assemble, organize, among others—citizens must also possess the minimal *resources* that are necessary in order to take advantage of the opportunities and to exercise their rights" (Dahl 2003, 152; emphasis in the original). One brief indication of just how skewed even *individual-level* campaign donations really are reveals that "of those who donated to presidential campaigns in 2000, 96 percent were white, 86 percent earned more than $100,000 a year, and 70 percent were male" ("On the Money Trail" 2004, 48).

Which Groups? Which Organizations? Who Decides?

If we were only concerned with the representation of narrow interests and particularity, then all this talk of groups would be misplaced—and I think it should be clear by now that I do not think this is the case. However, it does raise the specter of which groups, if we are to recognize them in some form, ought to count for special scrutiny, which organizations attempting to represent these groups should be publicly funded, who should make these decisions, and based on what criteria. Iris Marion Young has been roundly criticized (especially by those who are hostile to any form of group recognition at all, but also by those who are sympathetic) for not offering compelling enough grounds for establishing which groups should qualify for special representation rights. While this is an important and troubling complaint, I think it is often overstated.

Young argues that the groups that ought to count are those that have experienced an identifiable history of disenfranchisement—the effects of which remain evident in the forms of under-representation in legislatures, other representative bodies, and the mal-distribution of such social goods as solid educational opportunities, satisfying jobs, and high-quality housing. For example, fewer than half of black families own their own homes (compared with three-quarters of white families). This is primarily due to the fact that African Americans in 2002

> were 2.38 times as likely to have a mortgage application denied as were whites (up from 2.06 in 1997), and this disparity actually increases with income level: a low-income African-American is only 1.55 times as likely to be denied a mortgage as a low-income white, whereas an upper-income African-American is 2.83 times as likely to be turned down as a white of similar income. The good news: mortgage-denial rates for blacks overall have decreased (from 57 percent to 30 percent) since 1997, and the number of home loans blacks receive has increased (from 139,544 a year to 189,817). But 72 percent of this increase ACORN [Association of Community Organizations for Reform Now] points out, consists of higher-interest loans, suggesting not only that blacks will continue to be far less likely than whites to own homes, but also that those who do will be more heavily encumbered by debt. ("The Thick Red Line" 2004, 44)

Certainly the groups would be different in other regions of the world in which ethnicity or religion, for example, plays a more central role. Political and social conditions define group emergence and dissolution. Charles Tilly's most recent work on collective violence seeks, among other things, to explain why and how boundary activation (the us–them cleavage that is a central condition for the emergence of collective political violence) in a given social and cultural context erupts. He explains,

> [b]oth exploitation and opportunity hoarding gain in effectiveness when the categorical boundary in play corresponds precisely to a boundary that operates widely elsewhere in social life and thus brings with it a set of supporting beliefs, practices, and social relations. Boundaries of ethnicity, race, religion, gender, or nationality reinforce exploitation and opportunity hoarding. In their turn, exploitation and opportunity hoarding lock such differences in place by delivering greater rewards to occupants of the ostensibly superior category. (Tilly 2003, 10)

Although Tilly is making a general case for why certain types of collective political violence arise at certain periods under particular kinds of regimes, he explains how social, political, and economic boundaries emerge as the result of the seizure and (at least for a while) normalization of unequal shares of power and resources (i.e. through "exploitation" and "opportunity hoarding"). Under certain general conditions, those boundaries are activated, giving rise to identifiable forms of collective violence. "Thus, boundaries of sexual preference become more available for public political action in democracies than in nondemocracies, in so far as the people involved make their claims as categories of citizens deprived of equal rights rather than as separatist communities" (Tilly 2003, 76). The importance of Tilly for what I am trying to argue is that those cleavages betray the sites of inequality and can be identified by what groups in a society engage in sustained and often repeated collective political behavior, which can point to economic and political deprivations that correspond to those very cleavage lines.

When it is clear which larger groups will be recognized based on historical and ongoing marginalization, the next move will be to arrive at the precise organizations to which the public funding will go. Here I have in mind the creation of a congressionally appointed agency that would be responsible for making decisions about which organizations to fund as well as settling any disagreements about applying the criteria for qualifying as a disadvantaged group. Membership in the agency (let us call it the Agency for a Strong Democracy) would be contingent on a demonstrated commitment to full participation and would be up for review every four years.

Such an approach is reminiscent of the publicly funded community action program (CAP) created in the 1960s and 1970s through the Office of Economic Opportunity and under the auspices of the Economic Opportunity Act of 1964. Part of Lyndon Johnson's War on Poverty, the CAP was an attempt to enhance local control and increase political participation by injecting public resources into primarily urban communities. Although there were numerous failures associated with the CAP (not to mention its eventual gutting early in the Reagan administration) there were some notable successes in some cities in terms of increased public participation and positive policy change (Berry et al. 1993; Macedo et al. 2005).

I point to the CAP for a couple of reasons. First, when it was successful in particular cities, it was often so because the funding went directly to community organizations, bypassing the entrenched power of city councils, mayors, and local political party organizations (Berry et al. 1993, Chapter 2). It is partly because of the calcification of power inside local, state, and national party structures (along with the other reasons detailed in Chapter 3 and in the earlier portion of this chapter) that I am advocating something like alternative "shadow parties" to represent marginalized groups. However, this brings up two related and quite important issues: (1) what should these organizations do, and (2) how will the Agency for a Strong Democracy decide which organizations to fund?

The public provision of additional resources is necessary to both enhance the ability of existing organizations that are sometimes successful in achieving the outcomes favored by its members and supply incentives for the creation of new organizations that will be inclusive and responsive to regions and interests neglected by those existing organizations. Such public funding, coupled with more meaningful elections, would induce the members of disadvantaged groups to join together to engage in public participation and select slates of candidates that better reflect their interests and mobilize on their behalf. Ultimately the aim is to increase participation and, through that increased participation, develop participants' understanding of their interests and ability to communicate them more effectively.

The second related matter of how decisions will be made regarding which organizations will be funded is a substantial one. The primary concerns are that the funded organizations be able to demonstrate that they are representative of their membership and responsive to it. Funding would thus be dependent on grassroots support. Therefore organizations would essentially compete for support from the membership. Those organizations with the most support, demonstrated by either district-level voting or signature-gathering, would be funded for that cycle. Responsiveness would be addressed in ensuing funding cycles based on the past performances of the funded organizations. The number of organizations that exist at any one time that claim to represent a particular group could be rather numerous. Some will be overlapping in nature where multiple organizations share many of the same interests, but much of the multiplicity will be a reflection of differences in emphasis, approach, and even substantive claims within groups. It will be in the interests of the competing organizations, however, to eliminate duplicate organizations on the one hand, and on the other to reach out to those organizations where there exists the most common ground in order to pool support and have the most success in receiving funds and eventually electing preferable candidates. Some disagreements among organizations will not always be able to be accommodated, however, and in those situations, the Agency for a Strong Democracy will be instructed to fund multiple organizations based on demonstrated cleavages that for the time are unbridgeable.

The second key reason the community action program is relevant is that it demonstrates that it is not unrealistic to expect Congress to respond to issues of participation and representation. The citizen participation forged through CAP "was not forced upon Congress or agencies by a well-organized lobby that pushed strenuously for such programs" (Berry et al.1993, 35). Instead, efforts to increase public participation were enormously appealing particularly because of the "general feeling during the 1960's and 1970's that American democracy was sadly in need of reform. Rising levels of distrust in government, the domestic turmoil over the war in Vietnam, the disorder in the streets of Chicago during the 1968 Democratic convention, and the anger of blacks that had exploded into terrible riots" (Berry et al. 1993, 35) contributed to this feeling. The circumstances are currently quite similar in the United States. Presently there are widespread calls for fair elections, large majorities recognize a participation crisis, and serious distrust of the government is on the rise in light of activity undertaken in the guise of the war on terror (i.e. illegal domestic wiretapping, questionable public justifications for the invasion of Iraq, and the treatment of detainees), not to mention the most recent discovery of extensive money laundering and influence peddling by lobbyists and members of Congress. Citizens are pressuring Congress to at least respond to concerns about fair elections. However the response has been misplaced. Congressional action is this area has been primarily devoted to campaign finance reform, which has not only been a failure based on its purported goals, but even if successful would not remedy the true participatory woes that plague representative politics in the American context.

This does not mean that deciding which groups and organizations should be formally recognized will never be without controversy, but the criticism that it is eminently difficult to do so should no longer operate as a death knell. There will be controversy because citizens will disagree about whether and to what degree systemic inequality exists, especially based on particular group (rather than individual) distinctions, and what should be done to eliminate it. Groups should be able to demonstrate a history of *de jure* and/or ongoing practice of *de facto* inequality. They should be able to point to the ways in which certain social differences overlay squarely on multiple measures of social, economic, and political well-being (such as physical health, dignified jobs, and meaningful educational achievement). In other words, those groups that seek to make the case for why they should qualify for disadvantaged status should be able to demonstrate that on some key measures of well-being or human dignity the groups they represent tend to fall consistently on the losing side. Like Young, I agree that in the United States this will certainly mean that blacks, women, gays and lesbians, and Native Americans should qualify for federal funding.

For women, a particularly large and diverse group, this will mean that the pluralization of representation will be extremely important such that candidate slates and agendas that emerge from the organizations that represent them reflect relevant perspectives. It will also be the case, however, that women of color may find that their interests are better represented by organizations based on race or sexuality than on gender (or vice versa). Nothing prohibits participation in multiple organizations simultaneously.

Social class also presents a particular difficulty of size and diversity. Clearly unions operate to some degree as representatives of workers' interests and have secured for them an enormous bundle of rights, regulations, and provisions that would probably not have been adopted otherwise. However, many unions tend to be based on particular types of industry, and it does not seem likely that one union could effectively represent the myriad interests of "workers." While the working class is certainly a marginalized group and organizations that seek to represent working class interests could compete and be awarded public funding, I think social class is best represented indirectly through the groups who qualify for public funding—especially since issues of class cross-cut almost all the groups that would be likely to qualify for federal subsidization. It would be quite surprising indeed if class concerns did not arise among groups of Latinos, blacks, and women. In fact, when it comes to indicators of poor economic well-being (low pay, long hours, few if any benefits, and an inflexible labor schedule, for example), women and people of color assume a disproportionately large share. This disproportional result is precisely one of the prime indicators that systemic inequality exists. Furthermore, there is some direct recognition of class given that these groups must be *publicly funded* as a necessary, but not sufficient, condition of participating as equal citizens. Robert Dahl writes,

> James Scott has shown pretty convincingly that people who have been relegated to subordinate status by history, structure, and elite belief systems

> are much less likely to be taken in by the dominant ideology than members of the upper strata are prone to assume. *Given the open or concealed rejection of the elite ideology by members of the subordinate groups, a change in conditions, whether in ideas, beliefs, generations, structures, resources, or whatever, begins to offer the subordinate groups new opportunities to express their grievances.* And given these new opportunities and moved by anger, resentment, a sense of injustice, a prospect of greater individual or group opportunities, group loyalty, or other motives, some members of the subordinate groups begin to press for change by whatever means are available. Some members of the dominant group begin to support the claims of the subordinate strata. Privileged insiders ally themselves with outsiders. Insiders may do so for a variety of reasons: moral conviction, compassion, opportunism, fear of the consequences of disorder, dangers to property and the legitimacy of the regime arising from widening discontent, and even the real or imagined possibility of revolution. (Dahl 2003, 130; emphasis mine)

Thus a change in conditions, particularly (although not only) material conditions, directed at disadvantaged groups, which Dahl stresses throughout his evaluation of American democracy, is often the catalyst for political change. It is a change in conditions that can offer incentives for the marginalized to do things differently—for the costs of participation to be lowered and the benefits of engagement to be within reach.

A commitment to egalitarianism requires that some truly representative and deliberative body be entrusted to make these important decisions about which organizations should received funding. Thomas Christiano, who endorses a direct subsidy of the very kind I am proposing, explains that placing the power to decide on which groups count in the hands of the democratic legislature poses a problem of its own (Christiano 1996, 288–93). The problem is one of circularity, where we want democratic processes that produce democratic deliberative bodies, which then produce democratic processes. Why would we entrust a national legislative body to make decisions about which social differences should count when it is precisely that body that many have identified as patently unrepresentative? And if not the national legislature, then what other body would do? Can there be a way to intervene in this process that gives us what we want?

Christiano argues that, while this is a serious problem, it is not a problem distinctive to claims about special or group representation but rather a more general problem of democracy itself. "Democracy is hard to love," as Iris Young (2000, 16) keenly observes. We must continually work on developing fairer processes while using unequal outcomes as guides for informing procedural change. As I argued earlier, it is hardly unrealistic to expect Congress to respond to public pressure for reform. They have done so in the past when it came to measures to increase participation and representativeness. For the kind of public funding I am endorsing, it is impossible to bypass Congress altogether. While I am well aware of the potential problems posed by Congressional oversight, it is *precisely* this body that must be responsible for these decisions. It is Congress that, in taking up this charge, demonstrates the serious *public* commitment and social responsibility required to unravel inequality.

Conclusion

Does this not just take us back to the realm of pluralism with the representation of discrete interests and the same old pluralist dilemma of how we are to choose among so many aims and interests that are too often irreconcilable? However, democracy is not founded in a concern for maximizing social utility; instead it is based on the ideal of giving citizens equal control over their social world. Democracy distributes resources for controlling the social world, at least with regard to certain issues.

> democracy is not concerned with aggregating preferences; it is concerned with the distribution of authoritative power. The conception of a procedure is not aggregative; procedures are sets of rules used for distributing power. The equal distribution of authoritative power does not require that utility be maximized; these are two separate concerns. So that maximizing utility as it is construed by social choice theorists is incoherent and does not imply any incoherence in democratic ideals. (Christiano 1996, 96)

There are good indicators that the political processes we have in place, although seemingly neutral and thus equally applicable to all, have not provided and cannot provide the fair representation required for meaningful democratic practice. We must take social difference into account for fairness to obtain (Bickford 1999). Yet how we recognize difference so that it has an equalizing effect on participation and representation rather than an oppressive, ghettoizing one is of central importance.

Suzanne Dovi has recently written that the literature on group representation (primarily by feminist theorists) has focused on establishing the "*need for the presence* of some descriptive representatives, not on investigating *criteria for identifying preferable* descriptive representatives" (Dovi 2002, 729; italics in the original text). This silence has been justified, she argues, based on two arguments; one hailing from autonomy, the other from contingency. The autonomy argument posits that "members of historically marginalized groups should decide for themselves who is a preferable descriptive representative" (Dovi 2002, 732). Crafting a criteria *a priori* for evaluating descriptive representatives would thus violate and constrict the group's autonomy. This argument has two versions. "The first suggests that articulating criteria for judging descriptive representatives attributes to historically disadvantaged groups a fixed identity. The second emphasizes the autonomy of the representative" (Dovi 2002, 732). The contingency argument, on the other hand, alleges that "it is impossible to articulate the criteria that should be used to evaluate descriptive representatives because context matters" (Dovi 2002, 733). Neither of these broad arguments are convincing to Dovi. She writes,

> After all, to articulate such criteria is not necessarily to assume that all members of a historically disadvantaged group have some essential identity. In fact, the very real and politically relevant differences among members of historically marginalized groups point to the desperate need for a theoretical discussion of criteria. There is a difference between articulating particular policies that a descriptive representative must endorse to count as a legitimate descriptive representative and articulating guidelines for identifying preferable descriptive representatives. For instance, theorists of group representation have agreed that institutional reforms are necessary because historically disadvantaged groups possess overlooked interests. To maintain that a descriptive representative should pay special attention to overlooked interests does not require that she possess a particular view about those interests. (Dovi 2002, 734)

Thus she proposes a general criterion: "Democratic citizens should consider the degree to which a descriptive representative has mutual relationships with dispossessed subgroups as relevant to identifying preferable descriptive representatives. Preferable descriptive representatives will have strong *mutual* relationships with *dispossessed subgroups*" (Dovi 2002, 735; italics in the original text).

I agree with Dovi that sometimes fair representation requires descriptive representation and, furthermore, that there ought to be some criteria for evaluating to what degree fair representation is taking place. To a large extent, this chapter is an attempt to respond to the latter concern. While I have been critical of the adoption of reserved seats (particularly for its tendency to freeze difference) and party-list quotas (which are quite unlikely to be adopted in the United States), the evidence from around the world clearly indicates that the increased presence of female and minority candidates on ballots translates into their increased presence in representative bodies (Rule and Zimmerman 1994).

The most comprehensive data comes from the use of various forms of gender quotas. France, Argentina, South Africa, and Namibia have all adopted legislated quotas on party lists. Tanzania and India reserve seats for women: Tanzania reserves 20 percent of national seats and 25 percent of local government seats for women, while India reserves 33 percent of the seats for women at the local government level (Women in National Parliaments 2003).

More widespread is the adoption of voluntary quotas at the party list stage. Some examples of these include Sweden, Norway, Denmark, South Africa, Mozambique, Germany, and the UK. Not coincidentally, Sweden, Denmark, and Norway are among the top five nations globally when it comes to the highest percentages of women in national legislatures (Women in National Parliaments 2003).

One aspect of American exceptionalism overlooked by early American political development literature as discussed in Chapter 1 is our remarkably homogenous, status quo-oriented election procedures. Looking at how emerging and transforming democracies work to incorporate diversity might help observers in the United States envision viable alternatives, which assume diversity as a strength of democracy not a threat.

When it comes to translating heightened presence into relevant policy outcomes, we have to look no further than right here in the United States (see also Bowler et al. 2003, Rule and Zimmerman 1992, and Zimmerman and Rule 2000). In *After Suffrage: Women in Partisan and Electoral Politics before the New Deal*, Kristi Andersen (1996) debunks the previous conventional wisdom that women gaining the right to vote in 1919 made no appreciable difference in how politics was conducted or what policies were passed in the United States. In the years preceding women's enfranchisement (through informal means) and the three decades following it (through more formal procedures), women were instrumental in proposing and passing key pieces of legislation to protect gender rights (the Cable and Shepard–Towner Acts, for example), as well as the rights of the working class and children. In fact, much of that legislation was made possible through a form of group representation required within national party organizations, where first Democrats and later Republicans required gender representation on committees and delegate slates.

Deborah Stone has also pointed out that, in the American experience, the creation of alternative or parallel institution to represent weak interests has made a significant difference in fostering greater inclusion (Stone 2002, 362). Although by no means ushering in radical change, the creation of

> community action agencies did mobilize poor and minority constituencies to participate in elections, did recruit a large number of blacks, Hispanics, women, and other who had never been a part of government, did give them experience in running an agency and negotiating with other parts of government, and did force established political participants to deal with

> them. In 1965, there were seventy elected black officials at all levels of government in the United States, and those mostly on the lower levels. There were no black mayors. By 1981, there were 5,014 black officials, including mayors of 170 cities, many of whom had come up through the ranks of community action programs. The strategy of representing previously excluded groups in parallel institutions, then, does not cause a revolution, but it does integrate new groups into mainstream politics. (Stone 2002, 362–3)

Finally, many critics of coalition or consensual governments argue that majoritarian systems fare better when it comes to efficiency (arriving at decisions in a timely manner), stability, and overall domestic satisfaction. Non-majoritarian governments, on their account, ultimately frustrate democratic rule. However, it is not at all clear that majoritarian governments do, in fact, secure efficiency, stability, and citizen satisfaction (nor are these values the only ones, or even the most important, to which to hold a government) any better than consensual ones do. In Robert Dahl's most recent book, *How Democratic is the American Constitution?*, he argues that, while the United States is mostly a mixed government that exhibits aspects of majoritarianism, proportionality, and plurality, its *majoritarian* streak tends to discourage the achievement of democratic values—particularly the value of inclusion. He notes that

> [i]n a 1990 survey of citizens' views in eleven European democracies, respondents were asked how satisfied they were with "the way democracy works" in their country. They also reported how they voted in their country's last national election. Knowing the outcome of that election in each country, the authors of the study classified the respondents as winners or losers. The eleven countries were then arranged from the most majoritarian, Britain, to the most consensual, the Netherlands. The results, which the authors of the study describe as 'robust,' were pretty clear: In the more consensual countries, losers were almost as satisfied as the winners with the way democracy worked in their country. By contrast, in the more majoritarian countries, losers were much more likely to be dissatisfied. (Dahl 2003, 108; see also Lijphart 1984, 1999)

Thus, instead of majoritarian government making for a more satisfying, stable, and legitimate polity, it may well be that consensual, coalition-type governments fare noticeably better on such measures.

Based on the argument I have developed in the foregoing chapters, there is likely be a strong mutual relationship between the disadvantaged subgroup and its representatives if the candidates for election arise from those groups. Furthermore, such a preference for candidates rather than parties (or party lists) reinforces the mutuality Dovi is right in emphasizing, whereas a more party-centric system might well strengthen the parties' hold on nominations and agendas that would better develop from group members themselves. Additionally, holding a representative responsible for particular actions (or inaction) is also often easier to accomplish and recognize than doing so for an entire party.

Chapter 6
Social Class, Political Representation, and Democratic Revival: Resisting Quiescence and Manufactured Interests

Introduction

There has been much important work done in the past two decades on issues of under-representation in the American context based on social difference (Barry 2001; Benhabib 1996, 2002; Christiano 1996; Disch 2002; Gutman 1992; James 2004; Kymlicka 1995; Williams 1998). The relevant social differences include race, ethnicity, religion, class, gender, sexuality, and sometimes age. While this work has been particularly helpful in elucidating the ways in which women and racial, ethnic, and sexual minorities suffer disproportionately on measures of full citizenship, social class and culture receive relatively little attention in the American context. More often than not, social class and working class interests are swept in under the primary concerns of gender, race, and ethnicity. To a large degree, this weighting is understandable and justified based on clear and continued gender inequality as well as the legacy of slavery and centrality of race in America.

However, it strikes me that social class is neglected in American scholarship on political representation—something that cannot be said about the treatment of citizenship by scholars doing work on Latin America, France, Britain, and Canada, for example. This neglect is even clearer, for instance, given the utter lack of meaningful public dialogue about class or even a public language for addressing or conceiving of class interests that could be mobilized behind and formally represented in decision-making bodies. Furthermore, I find the claim that social class affects American public life relatively less than in these other countries both wrong and dangerous.

While these are important yet neglected dimensions of American social and political life, I argue that there are important links between social class and interests that reveal how class as a construction (no less than race and gender, for example) is fundamentally about power. I seek to examine the nature of those class-based relationships in order to elucidate more clearly my overall thinking about identity and why group-based representation rights are justified, indeed required, yet escape the essentialism associated with so much of the literature on group rights. In particular, I interrogate whether cultural difference (preferences, habits, dispositions, interests) is marked by class distinction and, if so, how? Is class defined and maintained, yet at the same time *masked*, by assigning social and cultural meaning to it? Probably it is some combination of the two. The answers to these questions are particularly important for what they reveal more broadly about the exercise of power in American politics; more specifically, insight into these relationships can provide valuable information about how to disrupt the cycle of systemic inequality. It is to these questions that I wish to turn in order to expand the scope of the project and increase the contribution that this work will make to the existing political science literature.

We are accustomed to the regular lamentations about the low levels of political participation in America. What is rarely part of this conversation is an acknowledgment that by participation we almost always mean voting, the thinnest form of political participation. Indeed, as Sheldon Wolin (2010) has recently remarked, voting simply substitutes for participation in a "managed democracy." Furthermore, there is virtually no public discussion that reaches large swaths of the citizenry that addresses the abject hollowness of casting a vote. The vote has been rendered practically meaningless because citizens have virtually no role in candidate selection. We employ a system of first past the post, single-member districts that encourages gerrymandering and depresses participation where there is little or no expectation that one's vote will be cast for a winning candidate. Furthermore, there is a widespread and well-founded sense that, regardless of who our representatives are, there will be no implementation of meaningful change that betters our lives. The *Citizens United* case that held that the First Amendment prohibits governmental limits on political expenditures by corporations and unions provides little reason to expect political participation in any form (other than corporate) to increase. It will probably continue to decline.

While voting clearly cannot be the stand-in for participation, it can be a powerful site of intervention for transforming government, fundamentally altering the agenda, and broadening the scope of politics. It is the construction of interests that will comprise the final section of the chapter. I am particularly interested in, on the one hand, examining how interests are manufactured, embraced, and internalized by citizens to neatly coincide with and reinforce corporate capitalist values as a stand-in for democratic norms. On the other hand, even when some citizens recognize these norms as deeply exploitive, there exists a deep and abiding sense of powerlessness and resignation—quiescence—that allows corporate power to set the agenda and manufacture almost unending yet meaningless choices within an unquestioned matrix of "free" market principles. It is the pervasiveness of this matrix (and a testament to its success) that has justified radically privatizing health, education, and military services, to name just a few. The overall effect is to emaciate the political—indeed even convince us of its nastiness, inefficiency, and powerlessness to render change.

Thus I am centrally concerned with suggesting practical yet powerful ways to go about increasing political participation through electoral reform, particularly by the poor and working class, women, and people of color while at the same recognizing that it cannot simply be a matter of getting more folks to vote and changing the legislative membership. It also has to be about broadening the scope and reach of politics to include meaningful democratic dialogue about strong egalitarianism and fairness as measures of right and justice rather than the market norms of a plutocracy.

Social Class and Political Representation

So what would all of this mean for the representation of the working class? By focusing on social class, I want to hone in on the ways in which the kind of group representation I am defending, and, maybe more importantly, the very justification I want to establish for designating such groups from the outset, is premised not on an assumption of shared interests and concerns based on essence but rather upon shared experiences of disregard, deprivation, and marginalization. While there are important differences in the ways in which race, ethnicity, sexuality, class, and gender are and have been constructed historically (especially at their intersections), all are products, at a very fundamental level, of the maldistribution of and struggle for power.

By carefully analyzing class, I hope to accomplish a couple of things. First, I hope to make it clearer that the social differences I am singling out for added scrutiny in representational politics are not based on any notion of a fixed and narrow set of interests shared by all members of the group. An emphasis on class allows me to make this case more clearly, since we are now somewhat less likely to ascribe class position to a natural or biological order than we are when it comes to race, ethnicity, sexuality, and gender. Second, class-based mobilization and representation is necessary for disrupting the cycle of systemic inequality perpetuated by a capitalist order. We cannot assume that this kind of intervention will take place as a result of mobilization by groups organized around race, ethnicity, gender, and sexuality, although it certainly could. In the absence of a significant place for class analysis, class interests, and class-based participation, these other groups will be prone to domination by their middle- and upper-class members. At the same time, class cannot be the central player that encapsulates concerns based on race, ethnicity, sexuality, and gender. Moving too far in that direction sets the stage for domination by the white working class. Instead, mobilization on all of these fronts will be necessary, but so too will be cooperation—at the very least to insure electoral success. However, cooperation should also begin to make greater sense when, through increased participation, citizens begin to see the links between class, race, ethnicity, sexuality, and gender.

Social Class and Power

When we talk about class, we generally focus on distinctions based on income. This measurement is problematic for a number of reasons. It generally ignores measures of wealth, disregards the uneven distribution of power that does not always co-vary with levels of income, and it distorts and masks the very maneuvers that construct social class in such a way to divide and suppress—indeed establish as simply unnecessary—any notion of working class interests, solidarity, and mobilization.

To be sure, there is great diversity within any measure of class. Class is cross-cut with gender, race, ethnicity, nationality, religion, sexuality, age, and more. There are also income and power differences within classes, although the differences between classes are significantly greater than those within. As I attempt to lay out a definition of social class based solidly on the differential access to power, it should be clear that I am not treating these categories as monolithic blocks but rather as relational categories that contain significant diversity within, yet whose members also share important interests in terms of gaining (or maintaining in the case of the capitalist class) meaningful influence over decision-making that affects and conditions their lives. I will also focus much more on the working class as both a political and an ethical move, very similar to Steve Bronner's notion of the "class ideal." He writes,

> Turning class into a primarily ethical notion, subordinating its economic to its political meaning, is a radical move. This does not involve simply forgetting about the empirical or structural elements of 'class.' But it does call for privileging the normative purpose of class analysis rather than simply engaging in empirical or structural investigations for their own sake. It highlights the need to resurrect the link between class analysis and class action. The class ideal speculatively projects the possibility of socialist practice and the preconditions for its success. Its metaphysical character thus retains a materialist purpose. Indeed, following Rousseau, the category seeks 'to unite what right sanctions with what is prescribed by interest, in order that justice and utility may in no case be divided.' (Bronner 1999, 326)

So who is the working class? Members of the working class are primarily marked by their relative lack of power and influence over their workaday lives, where they spend the majority of their time, and much of the rest of their lives as well—particularly in the realm of politics. As Michael Zweig notes,

> The working class is made of people who, when they go to work or when they act as citizens, have comparatively little power or authority. They are the people who do their jobs under more or less close supervision, who have little control over the pace or the content of their work, who aren't the boss of anyone. They are blue collar people like construction and factory workers, and white collar workers like bank tellers and writers of routine computer code. They work to produce and distribute goods, or in service industries or government agencies. They are skilled and unskilled, engaged in over five hundred different occupations tracked by the U.S. Department of Labor: agricultural laborers, baggage handlers, cashiers, flight attendants, home health care aides, machinists, secretaries, short order cooks, sound technicians, truck drivers. In the United States, working class people are by far the majority of the population. Over eighty-eight million people were in working class occupations in 2002, comprising 62 percent of the labor force. (Zweig 2004, 4)

Given the wide diversity of occupations sampled above, it should not be surprising that there is also income diversity as well. So how can they all be working class? By defining class on the basis of brute income (especially when we add wealth), glaring disparities are clear (and ever-expanding), which often signal structural inequality. However, such measures hide how important (to the workers) but ultimately negligible income differences outside the capitalist class do not translate into greater and more meaningful power and influence. In fact, it seems much more likely that the income differences in the working class serve to divide and placate it by preventing class consciousness from developing and providing some measure of disposable income that creates the illusion of prosperity and individuality. In fact, the very notion of the "middle class" serves precisely these functions. The vast majority of all Americans classify themselves as "middle class," regardless of their income levels on both the highest and even lower ends. However, when we think about class in terms of power instead of income or "lifestyle," the working class is significantly larger. Yet maybe more importantly, understanding class as a form of power forecloses the kind of thinking that dampens solidarity and mass participation and provides a meaningful basis for social action. If class conflict is framed and understood as a war declared by the poor against the rich, as the political right would have us believe, it is not likely to resonate with most Americans. "But if class conflict is represented as what it *is*, a contest of power to decide which interests will be served in the workplace and by public policy, a contest in which the interests of working people are different from those of capitalists, most Americans, and certainly most workers, get it" (Zweig 2004, 10).

Zweig continues:

> [c]lass divisions operate in public policy as well as in corporate structures. Classes can be found in the differential impact if such everyday elements as tax burdens, the pattern of government service cuts in a fiscal crisis, and the privatization of public services and imposition of markets and private enterprise for the provision of such basic services as healthcare and education. Class operates in regulatory policy and in government action (and inaction) related to collective bargaining and the ability of workers to organize unions. Class divisions even extend to foreign affairs, affecting the rules of international trade and investment, the structure of alliances, definitions of friend and foe, and the decision to make war. (Zweig 2004, 10)

To take this even further, cultures are also constructed and developed that map onto and give meaning to class divisions as well, so that, at a very deep level, how the relatively (much) less powerful think about who they are and what their positions are in the world is fundamentally structured and *naturalized* by tastes, preferences, practices, dispositions, and habits shaped and dictated by the voraciousness of the capitalist class. This notion is not dissimilar to Pierre Bourdieu's *habitus*—"systems of durable, transposable dispositions, structured structures predisposed to function as structuring structures, that is, as principles which generate and organize practices and representations that can be objectively adapted to their outcomes without presupposing a conscious aiming at ends or an express mastery of the operations necessary in order to attain them" (Bourdieu 1990, 53). He goes on to explain:

> The *habitus,* a product of history, produces individual and collective practices—more history—in accordance with the schemes generated by history. It ensures the active presence of past experiences, which, deposited in each organism in the form of schemes of perception, thought and action, tend to guarantee the 'correctness' of practices and their constancy over time, more reliably than all formal rules and explicit norms. This system of dispositions—a present past that tends to perpetuate itself into the future by reactivation in similarly structures practices, an internal law through which the law of external necessities, irreducible to immediate constraints, is constantly exerted—is the principle of the continuity and regularity which objectivism sees in social practices without being able to account for it; and also of the regulated transformations that cannot be explained either by the extrinsic, instantaneous determinisms of mechanistic sociologism or by the purely internal but equally instantaneous determination of spontaneist subjectivism. (Bourdieu 1980, 54)

What is particularly remarkable about the construction of social class is how invisible and thus durable it is—especially in the American context where the "individual" and "individuality" are paramount. The entire construction of social class is premised on the "free choices" of groups and individuals of pre-selected options that appear to be meaningfully different yet are anything but.

All of this is not to say that all working class folks enjoy bowling, domestic beer and not *too* foreign food. Rather at a more macro, structural level, tastes, preferences, and dispositions tend not to venture out beyond certain parameters; and those parameters are designed for selling and reinforcing particular understandings of oneself in the social order. They certainly tend not to venture into the realm of questioning market capitalism and the larger question of the overall distribution of power in the polity. Instead, choice, agency, and self-determination are defined by the seemingly endless manufactured options of consumerism and the perpetual valorization of "getting ahead."

Manufactured Interests, Quiescence, and Resistance

Our radically unequal yet durable distribution of wealth and power must be thoroughly cloaked in order to garner widespread acquiescence. Class denial, or the rejection of the existence of class boundaries or class immobility, is reflected in the very definition of the American experiment in democracy in the form of equality of opportunity. The Land of Opportunity cannot exist in the face of enduring and ever-widening class-based inequalities that, like race, gender, and sexuality, bear heavily on life chances. The identity of the nation reflected in its rhetoric and symbols and reinforced as a part of what passes as civic education (but is little more than hollow patriotism) is a powerful countervailing force. If what defines us (equal opportunity) is precisely what we lack, then the reality is too harsh to face, the blow to national and personal identity too much to bear. Thus any inequalities that cannot be effectively ignored must be shunted aside by claims of laziness, ignorance, and insufficient or incorrect morals and values, and the meanings of these claims are generally racialized and gendered as further evidence of how warranted the inequality actually is.

Citizens themselves then reinforce the legitimacy of the power order by internalizing those ideals and testifying to their achievement. Class denial is then also facilitated from the bottom up through the celebration of a voracious consumerism that provides access of large swaths of the citizenry to affordable (and often disposable) goods that tend to quickly morph into "necessities." For capitalism to continue to generate wealth in an era in which virtually all consumer markets have been tapped, the invention of new needs and desires becomes paramount—and all the better if those new needs can be perpetually satisfied with replacement goods, because the previous ones were not built to last or because of planned obsolescence. It becomes increasingly difficult, then, to allege class immobility and deprivation when so many things can be had and enjoyed. This is a thin satisfaction, however—bread and circuses—to placate and divert attention away from the broader power scaffolding that determines what is available for public decision-making.

Understanding class as an exercise in power sets the stage for revealing how citizen interests are often systemically manufactured so as to reinforce the existing power order. I want to suggest that citizen interests are often deeply influenced by social and political context, and that context is defined and legitimized by a certain distribution of power made possible by the embrace of market capitalism and the foregrounding of corporate norms such as profit, efficiency, and expansion. It is interesting, although not surprising, that scholars of political representation tend to take citizen interests at face value. Questioning citizens' stated preferences implies that there are objective ones separate from citizen claims—an implication that smacks of elitism and anti-democratic overtones.

To say that there are interests that are roughly objective, however, does not necessarily mean that most citizens are ignorant or dupes regarding their desires, wants, and conceptions of a meaningful life. I am using interests here in a broader, distinctly political fashion as a set of ideas about how power is exercised and negotiated—interests as a means to an almost unlimited variety of ends. What it is to live a meaningful life, to possess and enjoy something like self-realization, can take any number of forms. However, being able to achieve, much less even *conceive* of, the rich variety of options available is foreclosed where interests are the product of a pre-selected set of options that conform to capitalist values as the replacement for democratic ones. So it is not that we are simple victims of a swindle. Throughout this project I have been addressing the existence of social difference as a way of justifying differential access to power. Interests are no different. If how we think about ourselves and how we are perceived by others is profoundly influenced by social and political context, what we regard as being in our best interests surely cannot fail to be similarly conditioned. When that context is defined by a set of corporate, capitalist norms that are increasingly substituting for democratic values, the interests that make the most sense, that have the most resonance, are the ones that confirm the existing arrangement of things. What makes this phenomenon even more powerful and resistant to change is that it reinforces the ongoing starvation of the political. Indeed there is less and less need for a contentious politics that challenges the status quo when the way things are done might only need the occasional tweak. Thus one outcome is a certain satisfaction with current arrangements.

Of course this is not the only result. As Steven Lukes (2004) and John Gaventa (1982) (among others) have pointed out, it is not always the case that lack of mobilization or easily visible resistance in a context of social and political deprivation translates into contentment. Rather it is more often the case, especially in the cases of deep deprivation, that it is not contentment but quiescence—a sense of resignation that, while life conditions are poor and even desperate, politics is not a feasible avenue for rectifying these ills.

Manufactured interests are thus a set of dense but expansive norms that serve as the scaffolding for a particular understanding of power. This creates a mirage of the realm of power as broadly accessible and diffused. Citizens tend to either take on these interests as their own or reject them but acquiesce. Resistance occurs at the margins, of course, and occasionally erupts with greater collective force, but these challenges almost always result in minor changes (sometimes with meaningful results for how people live their lives, for sure) that do little if anything to alter practices at the structural level. Manufactured interests are not the false preferences or wants of a duped citizenry but the internalization of a certain understanding of power that structurally impedes and often completely forecloses the achievement of real emancipation and human agency.

The social difference that I foreground in much of this project is, like class difference, created to legitimize the existing distribution of power. That power is divided and normalized through a synchronous relationship between capitalism and a set of gendered and racialized norms. Those norms or deep assumptions about race, gender, and nation work to effectively cloak the capitalist generation of inequality while at the same time serving as justifications for capitalist expansion and imperial politics. If we are going to be serious about political representation, we have to be acutely aware of the ways in which interests are the product of not just the experience of social difference as traditionally understood, but also the result of the inculcation and prioritization of market capitalist values. A broader recognition by members of the working class of the structural reality within which interests are manufactured will provide a basis for resistance and mass mobilization toward a fairer democratic order. This will certainly not be an easy or rapid development. Nevertheless, I would like to suggest two potentially powerful sites for cultivating the skills and space for democratic transformation.

Transforming Social Processes: Education

Electoral reform will not, of course, cure all the ills that plague political representation. Along with electoral reform must come a genuine commitment to develop and sustain a more democratic political culture. This will require greater opportunities and spaces for citizens to learn about the issues that affect them, gain insight into more effective ways to convey their interests to others, set the agenda, deliberate, and acquire some power over the decisions and processes that affect their lives. There are innumerable prescriptions proposed by theorists and activists to develop such spaces and habits. Here I want to focus on public education and the workplace—two powerful sites for the production of manufactured interests and thus crucial locations for fomenting resistance.

The work of Frances Fox Piven (2006), Piven and Richard Cloward (1979) and James Scott (1985, 1990) has been deeply influential to social scientists who deal centrally with the workings of power. I highlight them specifically because, when joined together, their analyses reveal evidence of counter-hegemonic practices and discourse among ordinary people that, while often hidden, serve as the repository of grievances, anger, and resistance that can, under ripe conditions, develop into collective disruption—very much like what we have seen in Wisconsin in response to the drastic measures taken by Governor Scott Walker targeting working people and seeking to eliminate unions in that state by eroding collective bargaining rights.

While I do not dispute the hidden transcript that testifies to the existence of a counter-narrative and individual forms of resistance that can turn into collective disruption for egalitarian reform, those times of reform are few and far between and gains are often systematically rolled back in the long "in-between" periods, as Piven clearly explains (2006). Maintaining the hidden transcript is an act of resistance in itself, and often physically and psychically labor-intensive, although it can certainly be nourishing as well. This scholarship is thus both heartening and crushing at the same time. It demonstrates that ordinary citizens recognize the power structure within which they are enmeshed and resist it in ways that the powerful tend not to detect readily. It also points out how collective disruption has been the key force behind egalitarian reform in the United States. What this scholarship also reveals is that collective resistance is far from common and that reforms are fairly easily eroded. Indeed what it *does not* tell us is how widely shared the counter-hegemonic narratives are and who among us is cognizant of them. The work of Piven (2006), Piven and Cloward (1979) and Scott (1985, 1990) seems to indicate that, while collective disruption happens and is a powerful, indeed key, force for more just practices and policies, not all citizens share a recognition of or access to the story about power contained in the hidden transcripts. Buying into the dominant story about equality of opportunity and the freedom and potential security offered by free markets is deeply attractive. This attractiveness is developed and reinforced earliest in the public schools.

Indeed, public schools are the central site for inculcating market values as *the* measuring stick against which the good is judged. While there is substantial literature that addresses the relative worth of what, substantively, we teach in the classroom, and the implications of those choices, I want to suggest that a greater emphasis on developing critical thinking skills and encouraging a healthy skepticism is a necessary addition to a democratic pedagogy. Employing something like the community action program model that I endorse in the previous chapter to address doling out resources for electoral organization and mobilization, similar grants should be allocated by the federal government and distributed to municipalities precisely for local education reform. Such funds might encourage greater experimentation and shake up school board membership. Agitating for curricular change that encourages critical writing and research skills can also avoid some (certainly not all) of the treacherous, politically charged battles over content.

Teaching students how to read carefully and critically, and analyze what they read from an early age is critical. Learning how to find information, contextualize concepts, and assess sources is essential. These skills are *citizenship* skills. In order for citizenship to be a meaningful measure of democracy, we cannot simply speak in terms of equal voting rights and membership in the polity. Citizenship must also be measured by *democratic agency*—the possession of a critical consciousness developed through public schooling as part of an investment in civic education—not separated out into civics lessons but critical thinking itself as a civic virtue. This must be a public commitment because it is a democratic one. A people who possess more than a bundle of membership rights but also real agency to exercise those rights in a critical fashion to alter agendas and ultimately expand the political in ways that reflect citizens' interests is a people with power.

Citizen/Worker

Such opportunities to participate will be especially important in the workplace, given its importance in our lives. Robert Dahl puts it best when he writes,

> Work is central to the lives of most people. For most people, it occupies more time than any other activity. Work affects—often decisively—their

> income, consumption, savings, status, friendships, leisure, health, security, family life, old age, self-esteem, sense of fulfillment and well-being, personal freedom, self-determination, self-development, and innumerable other crucial interests and values. Of all the relations of authority, control, and power in which people are routinely involved, none are as salient, persistent, and important in the daily lives of most persons as those they are subject to at work. (Dahl 1989, 327)

If work occupies so much of our lives and informs to a large extent much of what our lives consist, then so long as the workplace remains non-democratic and even despotic, we can expect members of the polity to behave primarily as consumers and subjects. As Murray Edelman illustrates, systems of power create a context within which the privileged control the terms of debate. It is the workplace that takes over from public education the reinforcement of the context that establishes a key set of norms and values within which decision-making occurs. The workplace looms large in our lives not only because of how much time it consumes and our dependence on wages; it is also a potent contributor to how we think about ourselves and are regarded by others. It plays an enormous role in the framing of social reality. Thus it does at least double duty in contributing mightily, at the macro-level, to the norms and values that determine the contours and reach of the political while inculcating, at the micro-level, the virtue of those very same norms and values in individuals through the disciplining power of work.

Of course these aren't just any norms being reinforced in the workplace but the market norms that facilitate capitalist exploitation and social and economic stratification. In order for these norms to operate effectively in the face of radical inequality, there has to be fairly substantial faith in corporate capitalism and the paper-thin liberal democracy that provides its political cover. In the small pockets of the populace where that faith does not exist, the structure of corporate, capitalist democracy is expansive and strong enough to generally evince quiescence. The fact that there is no sustained critique of capitalism shared by anything like a significant number of citizens in the United States points to a combination of begrudging acceptance and significant internalization. Of course citizens critique and resist unjust outcomes, but the degree to which they ascribe them to systemic causes remains extremely low.

The exceptions are vital, however. Periods of economic and political crisis reveal fissures and failures in the dominant narrative. Those who have been active resisters but on the margins are joined by the previously quiescent and increasingly by those who had bought into the equal opportunity mantra but find it no longer sustainable. This was the case in the major egalitarian reform movements of the twentieth century in America: the labor movements of the late nineteenth and early twentieth centuries opened up by rapid industrialization and market failure, the first wave of the women's movement and abolition, and the Civil Rights Movement, among others.

The latest economic crisis is again opening up possibilities for critique and resistance. Not only do crises of this sort reveal cracks in the capitalist hegemony, but they also create space for reformers and challengers to contend over policy and agendas while revitalizing politics as a meaningful site for challenging power. As the number of our nation's unemployed (and underemployed and those who have simply given up) continued to rise, millions of families lost their homes to foreclosure (mostly because of vastly over-priced real estate and subprime lending made possible by decades of federal deregulation of the banks), and wages remained stagnant at best, Governor Scott Walker of Wisconsin proposed a radical set of measures to control spending and reduce the debt. These proposals had nothing to do with creating security for an already desperate populace by increasing revenue from those who are most able to pay but generally pay a lower rate than the middle class or none at all (see the Office of Management and Budget 2010). Instead Governor Walker took this opportunity to go after public employee unions by slashing pay, benefits and, most notably, collective bargaining rights—the very heart of organized labor and a real coup for corporate power if achieved. What is interesting is that this dramatic overreach at a time of great economic desperation and uncertainty touched off a resistance movement in Wisconsin that served as a touchstone for mass mobilizations in as many as 40 other states. Governor Walker's move is emblematic of aggressive moves in other states to further cripple organized labor and other pockets of popular resistance.

Walker's move might ironically enough have been the very jolt needed to energize forms of collective resistance that stem directly from labor practices. Because the target of Walker's proposals was not simply the middle and working classes but people power itself in the form of collective bargaining, it became broadly apparent how the powerful were seeking to exploit the economic crisis (a crisis brought on, in fact, by decades of federal policy reflective of corporate interests). This is an important part of why the movement was not confined to Wisconsin. Indeed such acts at the state level along with federal policy regarding lending and taxation helped to spawn the Occupy Movements. What began as Occupy Wall Street, a popular push-back in response to decades of federal policy that dramatically increased corporate power, quickly morphed into local and state-based Occupy mobilizations. Local community activists took over public parks throughout the country, demanding economic and political reforms—indeed most found themselves fighting for the very right to remain in those parks as an act of protest. It remains to be seen how enduring or successful the Occupy movement will be, but one of its strengths thus far is its diffuse organizational structure, which allows for quick adaptation to policy proposals and tactical innovation.

The workplace defines us in fundamental ways and it is where we spend so much of our adult lives. It is useless to speak of living a dignified life without having meaningful work, and the crucial first element of meaningful work is having a say in how that work is to be conducted, organized, and remunerated. Real collective bargaining is a partnership based on our equal humanity. We cannot be citizens in the political sphere while subjects in the labor force. We cannot hold out much hope that individuals will engage the world as agents of political change so long as such power goes unrecognized and unchecked. Democratizing the workplace could very well serve as a democratic laboratory that not only produces goods and services but also cultivates engaged, efficacious citizens.

Political Participation and Representation

Participation must always be the other side of representation, as meaningful political representation only has significance when informed by broad-based political engagement. Yet the shrinking of the political and thus the reach of democratic decision-making has schooled citizens in the ways of isolation, passivity and apathy. Extending the reach of democracy to realms such as the workplace will go a long way towards educating individuals about what it means to be a citizen (Pateman 1970). Individuals will begin to see themselves as real agents rather than passive recipients of demands and advertising campaigns. For

> one's recognition of oneself as a person with aims worth pursuing depends on one's having some significance for others. We depend crucially on the esteem and respect of others to have a conception of ourselves as worthy persons. If nothing one does commands respect from others or moves others to act on a voluntary basis, one's conception of oneself will be incapacitating. One will lack the self-confidence and the sense of the worth of one's projects necessary for full personhood. The respect and esteem one needs from others can only be provided if they share an equal status with oneself. (Christiano 1996, 29)

When individuals regard themselves as citizens, as real agents, they are more likely to participate in public affairs. That participation is more likely to be sustained, furthermore, when the processes in which they engage are fair and yield results. Crigler, Just, and McCaffery in a very recent study have added to the empirical evidence that indicates that the type of electoral formula affects participation, "with proportional representation systems generating higher voter participation than majoritarian or plurality elections" (Crigler, Just, and McCaffery 2004, 138; see also Blais and Dobrzynska 1998; Jackman 1987; Jackman and Miller 1995; Ladner and Milner 1999; Powell 1986). They continue,

> [m]otivational explanations focus on the differential incentives facing citizens under alternative electoral arrangements. Under majoritarian systems, such as first-past-the-post used for the House of Representatives in the United States Congress, Westminster, and states employing unit rule for votes in the Electoral College, supporters of minor and fringe parties like the Greens—whose geographic support is dispersed widely but thinly across the country—may feel that casting their votes will make no difference to who wins in their constituency, still less to the overall composition of government and the policy agenda. (Crigler, Just, and McCaffery 2004, 138)

We know, furthermore, that members of less privileged groups participate at far lower rates than those who are privileged by their race, class, ethnicity, and gender (Burns, Schlozman and Verba 2001 and 1997; Verba et al. 1993; Verba, Burns and Schlozman 1997; see also Bennett and Resnick 1990). Not only do members of these less privileged groups participate at significantly lower levels than their white, middle- and upper-class male counterparts, but their lack of participation matters, as women, African-Americans, and Latinos do "differ in their attitudes on political matters, partisan affiliations, vote choices, and needs for government policy" (Verba, Schlozman and Brady 1995). Verba et al. write that their analysis

> has shown that although similar in their preferences as measured by standard NES attitude questions, citizens who are active and those who are not are quite different in their demographic attributes, their economic needs, and the government benefits they receive. These disparities are exacerbated when we move from the most common political act, voting, to acts that are more difficult, convey more information, and exert greater pressure. With respect to the volume of activity, the disparity is especially great for electoral contributions: the advantaged account for the overwhelming share of the dollars donated to campaigns … In terms of a set of issues of particular salience to those who are economically disadvantaged, namely, concerns about basic human needs, the disadvantaged speak with a distinct voice. Not only do such issues weigh more heavily in their lists of concerns, but when they communicate about these matters to public officials, they are more likely to be discussion issues that touch their own lives and more likely to be prescribing greater public attention to these needs. (Verba et al. 1993, 313–14)

There is a fairly substantial body of empirical literature, which Verba et al. (1993, 303) discuss, concluding that "demographic characteristics are a very imperfect predictor of either their policy preferences or their behavior in office" (see also De la Garza 1995). What their study reveals, however, is a more complex but complete picture that shows the extent to which democratic representation is taking place. They do this by looking beyond the correspondence (or lack thereof) between stated voting and policy preferences and policy outcomes. They look to other forms of political participation, such as working for a campaign, making a campaign contribution, joining a group to pressure elected officials, phoning representatives, and attending demonstrations.

Furthermore, they supplement pre-selected and closed-ended policy preference options on the survey with open-ended queries. Their approach revealed a participation and representation gap that before had gone unrecognized. They found that, "with respect to socio-economic status (income and education), the activity disparities among groups are much more substantial … and … those differences imply that those who would be most in need of government response because they are dependent on government programs are the least likely to make themselves visible to the government through their activity" (Verba et al. 1993, 305). In fact, compared with the economically advantaged, the disadvantaged (particularly those who receive means-tested benefits), are four times as likely "to have been animated by concerns about basic human needs, such as poverty, jobs, housing, and health" (Verba et al. 1993, 311–12). They conclude,

> With respect to concerns about basic human needs, information-rich forms of participation carry different kinds of messages from different groups. The issue-based activity of the disadvantaged and recipients of means-tested government benefits is more likely to be inspired by such concerns. However, because these groups are less active, they actually send fewer messages about basic human needs than do more advantaged respondents. The communications from the advantaged differ in two fundamental ways from those sent by the disadvantaged. First, the advantaged are much less likely to be discussing problems that they experience in their own lives. In addition, policy statements from the advantaged are not uniformly supportive of greater efforts to meet problems of basic human needs. (Verba et al. 1993, 313)

While participation rates vary among disadvantaged groups, Verba, Schlozman, and Brady (1995, 355) have demonstrated that "*differential access to the resources that foster participation*" (emphasis mine) is one of the prime reasons for the participation gap. In a later study, Burns, Schlozman, and Verba

Second, I find the concept of political race as a tool for diagnosing systemic inequality and providing a basis for cooperation and collective action across traditional identity boundaries attractive. However, it neglects, in important ways, questions related to gender and sexuality, for example, that can operate in ways that race, even political race, does not—rendering it suspect in its ability to even diagnose systemic inequality not to mention the difficulties entailed in forging cooperation across race and class lines but also across lines related to gender and sexuality that those marginalized on the basis of race or class might not be willing to reach across. I think such cooperation can in fact be forged, but political race remains partial in so far as it fails to engage these differences. While I agree with Guinier that race can be a powerful lens through which to identify systems of power, I think her honing in on race has something to do with an already existing repository of race-conscious jurisprudence from which she can draw.

Another example helps illustrate these limitations. Guinier argues that districting, and particularly race-conscious districting, is problematic because it is premised on an assumption that citizens in a given geographic region share some set of interests that can then be represented by a single elected official (or can be virtually represented by an official in another district). This assumption is flawed because citizens do not move to districts but to neighborhoods, and those neighborhoods are often structured by race and class. However, even this structuring does not imply shared values (even if we draw, as we have in some instances, district lines along such boundaries). We have been and should be attempting to represent interests, according to Guinier. We have simply gone about it in the wrong way. On this count, I agree with Guinier. Part of her justification for representing interests (rather than defined groups) is that she is clearly concerned about cross-cutting memberships. On the other hand, she recognizes that under-represented social groups in fact exist and ought to find ways in which to organize and agitate for better representation, but she rejects group-specific proposals that would grant resources for precisely these purposes. There are ways, and Iris Young is particularly helpful here, to develop group-specific, quasi-institutional measures that can improve the representation of marginalized groups without bowing to essentialism. However, acknowledging these very real concerns, Guinier's focus on race (to the exclusion of gender and sexuality in particular) and interests, both of which are important, is at least partially the result of her centering of the law in which race and interests already enjoy legal precedent.

Moreover, the concept of political race of Guinier and Torres can serve as a powerful diagnostic tool when it comes not only to race, but also class. In fact, the axis of race and class (blacks and poor whites, for example) forms much established that, in accounting for the gender gap in political participation, socio-economic resources were quite important. "Women are, on average, disadvantaged with respect to education, income, and occupational status, attributes long known to be associated with political activity. These deficits are important in accounting for the participation gap. In particular, the disparity in educational attainment is significant in accounting for gender differences in participation" (Burns, Schlozman, and Verba 2001, 359–60).

Thus if some minimal level of resources is necessary for the exercise of basic democratic rights, then the provision of those rights is a social obligation. Alleviating this participation disparity is not simply a problem of gathering all relevant information and interests so that policy outputs are "better." Rather, "*political equality* will require that the resources for participating in social deliberation be equally distributed" (Christiano 1996, 43; emphasis mine).

Social Class, Political Participation, and the Expansion of the Political

Class is constantly constructed and reconstructed to maintain the power order. So long as its power dimensions remain opaque to citizens, there is no real hope of meaningful class-based mobilization. The kind of electoral reform I advocate, cumulative voting in significantly larger, multi-member districts coupled with federal funding of historically marginalized groups for self-organization, mobilization, and the nominating and running of slates of candidates that reflect the members' interests, could serve working class interests well—provided that the incentives for mobilization are strong. In this kind of electoral scheme, working class interests, among the interests of other disadvantaged groups, would be less likely to be shunted to the side, since electoral success (gaining enough seats to effect meaningful policy change) would require significant coalition-building and strategic voting. However, it is likely that mass participation by the working class will require more than federal funding and a greater possibility of electoral success (although these are of central importance).

In addition to these necessary measures, there must be a greater awareness of the construction of class—how it is created and masked and for what purposes—in order to disrupt the cycle of systemic inequality. This critical consciousness must come about at the grassroots level among those who are already organized or are organizing at the local level. It can certainly take place within labor unions (although their power has diminished significantly over recent decades, and their agenda of labor reform, while important, is only one part of the kind of transformation that must occur at the structural level). It could occur on college campuses and in community centers and prisons. It must also occur in the popular media. Numerous articles in the *New York*

Times, on-line sites such as *Slate*, and newspapers and newscast across the nation report fairly regularly now on the increasing gap between the wealthiest Americans and the working poor. Indeed, it is remarkable how large the gap has become between the "ultra-wealthy" and the just "run-of-the-mill wealthy." In 2006, the *New York Times* reported on the growing phenomenon of the "ghetto tax"—higher rates paid by the generally urban poor for car insurance (for identical cars), appliances and furniture from "rent to own" stores, and groceries, for example. In April 2006, Walter Kirn, writing in the *New York Times Magazine*, notes how, as the gap between rich and poor has grown, we seem to have no vocabulary with which to talk about it since "wealth" and "poverty" meant something different in the 1970s. Wealthy previously meant "millionaires" (we still make this reference), he notes, although many of the wealthy are closer to billionaires (Kirn 2006, 12). "Poor," too, no longer means something straightforward, according to Kirn. He goes on to observe that "the nonsimple words are taking over. The words with 11 bedrooms and 7 baths that are larger and finer than rich folks needed before the 'differentiation'—which isn't merely an economic trend but a style, an aesthetic. Since the early 1980's on, Secretary [of the Treasury John] Snow said, 'we've seen a rise in inequality, but we've also seen parallel to that a continuous rise in living standards.' To know what he means, you would have to read the studies, but to know how he feels, you just have to hear his diction. To my ear, the man sounds satisfied. And convinced that his listeners should be satisfied too" (Kirn 2006, 12). It is precisely this kind of sentiment voiced so matter-of-factly and reasonably by Snow that must be resisted and unmasked. So too the analysis of David Brooks in a recent *Times* op-ed in which he laments the declining work ethic and moral fiber of the working class. "For the first time in history," he writes, "the rich work longer hours than the proletariat" (Kirn 2006, 11). This was following a front-page *Times* piece a few days earlier, and cited by Brooks, about a growing percentage of middle-aged men who have dropped out of the labor force, preferring to read, write novels, and pursue other various hobbies (excepting those who dropped out for health reasons), while diminishing their savings. He judges this occurrence as a "migration of values" (Kirn 2006, 11). Where middle-class men once "defined their dignity by their ability to work hard, provide for their family and live as self-reliant members of society," they now define their dignity "the same way the subjects of Thorstein Veblen's *Theory of the Leisure Class* defined theirs" (Kirn 2006, 11). What of dignity being defined by a fair wage, democratic decision-making in the workplace, universal health coverage, and a safe environment in which to labor—much less meaningful and fulfilling labor? If we understand and begin to converse about class as a construction informed, conditioned, and maintained by a corporate, capitalist power order and not simply represented by income, wealth, and personal possessions, then these kinds of attacks and misrepresentations become much clearer as the machinations that serve to maintain the current state of inequality and injustice. Such an environment could foster what Doug McAdam calls "cognitive liberation" that is necessary to fuel the kind of political participation—indeed mass mobilization—that is the necessary precursor of and corollary to fair political representation.

Chapter 7
Conclusion: A Feminist Politics of Inclusion

Over the past 15–20 years, in both politics and the academy, matters of social difference have assumed a prominent place. Evidence of this manifests itself in questions over the worth and necessity of Affirmative Action policies in hiring and higher education, the prudence of racial and political gerrymandering, the justifiability of restricting social services to only US citizens, and the fairness of limiting marriage to heterosexual couples. Scores of books from the academy address how and to what degree "identity" markers (such as race, class, ethnicity, and sexuality) describe something meaningful about how individuals negotiate their lives (and indeed what kinds of lives they live), and what can and should be done to ameliorate unfair causes and outcomes. While I have attempted neither to address nor to solve all of these problems, what I have tried to do is make the case that some differences do matter, and the only way to arrive at fair (if temporary) solutions that we all must abide by is for the decision-making process to include representatives that reflect all the relevant interests and concerns of the polity.

The central dilemma as I see it is how to increase the representation of those citizens whose membership in some group (or even more likely a series of groups) has rendered them systemically under-recognized in the polity—but in such a way that minimizes the tendency to freeze differences and demand assimilation. Feminist theory is essential for understanding not simply that the historically disenfranchised need to be enveloped into the democratic fold. Rather it has been indispensable in unmasking the "universal" conceptions of the citizen, politics, and representation, to name only a few, as imposters that in fact reflect the experiences of a minority of the democratic community. The growing literature on intersectionality has been particularly important in this regard. Kimberlé Crenshaw (1995, 1998) and Lynn Weber (2001) clearly demonstrate in their work how the experiences of black women are effectively erased in the conception and application of anti-discrimination legislation. Patricia Hill Collins (2000) reveals the ways in which gender and race intermingle such that the options for what it means to be a black woman are often confined to passive maternalism (mammies), emasculating and castrating dominators (matriarchs), or over-sexualized harlots (hot mammas). Yet given that feminist theory is so necessary for interrogating such constructions and the

Table 7.1

Scholar	Identity/difference	Representation	Participation	Remedy
Guinier	Foregrounds race but neglects gender and sexuality (and to a lesser degree class)	Of interests (which can be attached to social groups, but the attachment is too loose for representation purposes) *Rejects "group representation"*	*Moderate*: encourages participation based on "political race"	Electoral reform (cumulative voting in multi-member districts) and enhanced participation through "political race"
Phillips	Foregrounds gender but neglects race and ethnicity	Of preferences and ideas (which are not necessarily attached to social difference—certainly not enough to justify "group representation" in the strong sense) *Rejects "group representation"*	*Moderate*: funnels participation primarily through party politics	Party list quotas for gender parity and "targets" for racial and ethnic minorities
Young	Valorizes social difference to the detriment of important intra-group cleavages	Of social perspectives (where interests and preferences are tightly attached to social difference) *Endorses "group representation"*	*Moderate*: focuses on deliberation in representative bodies	Representation of social perspectives in representative bodies operating under fair and open deliberative conditions
Inclusive representation	Recognizes the importance of cross-cutting identities and allegiances (by encouraging organization membership based on self-identification)	Of interests (which are understood to be tied to social difference but not only in one direction) *Endorses recognition of groups for public funding and mobilization*	*Strong*: emphasizes the importance of public funding of marginalized groups for initiating and sustaining meaningful participation	Electoral Reform with publicly funded national elections and public funding for disadvantaged groups to organize and select slates of candidates and influence agendas and policy

policies and practices upon which they are founded, what insights, in particular, does it afford for the representation of these historically marginalized groups?

The feminist theorists analyzed here each contribute insight into a blended theory of fair and inclusive political representation. Table 7.1 sketches a comparison of the approaches of Lani Guinier, Anne Phillips, Iris Marion Young, and myself (inclusive representation) on central dimensions of the representation of historically disadvantaged groups. A narrative explanation follows.

Guinier points us to the ways in which legal and institutional interventions can be made in the here and now (both top-down and bottom-up). If we care, as we ought to, about representing interests and making votes count, then Guinier's critique of single-member geographic districting as a poor proxy for the representation of interests illustrates the necessity of instituting a system of representation within multi-member districts that employs cumulative voting. Such a system, accompanied by a breaking down of traditional identity lines that have a tendency to pit groups against one another rather than encourage alliances, should go a long way toward increasing participation and making the vote a more robust democratic tool. Nevertheless, Guiner's theory of representation is partial in at least two important ways. I think this is primarily because of her law-centered analysis. First, her emphasis on the law leads in rather clear ways to a concentration on institutional reforms that can be accommodated by American jurisprudence. In many ways this is positive, since it provides us with realistic goals and practical channels for pursuing those goals. However, I think her focus on the law limits her ability to imagine reforms that could take place (and ought to take place) beyond strict legal practice. For example, cultivating community ties (through the creation of more public spaces and new urban and neighborhood development that encourages community involvement and contact) fosters solidarity across the distinctions of difference that can then begin to dissolve the notions of fixed identity that we assign groups on the margins. We can then recognize them as political and social constructions developed to maintain and nourish a system of privilege and power.

Guinier's donning of the lens of the law also confines her understanding of American jurisprudence as a much more static, inelastic institution than it actually is. I think this is, at least partially, why she refuses to advocate group-specific policies like public funding for organization (beyond her concerns about cross-cutting memberships). The law, on her account, is simply not equipped in the American context for such strong accommodation of groups.

of the foundation for their argument. They provide convincing evidence that blacks, Hispanics, and poor whites, upon recognizing their linked (structured) existences, can and do find a basis upon which to cooperate. Beyond that diagnostic stage, however, Guinier and Torres have little to say about *how* that cooperation and participation will come about. If we really care about social class, there is a very real need for the provision of public funds to foment self-organization and mobilization. For Guinier, the question that drives her analysis is, *"How can electoral reform be meaningful?"*

Phillips adds gender in a central way that Guinier does not—as well as economic considerations and how they are inextricably tied to political recognition as well as social well-being. While I think that she is right to criticize Young for granting a veto power, she does not go far enough to empower the marginalized, because she privileges a certain understanding of equality. Phillips rejects "group rights" because they offend the ideals of fair treatment upon which merit and equal opportunity rest. However, there are less institutionalized or stringent ways of recognizing groups, such as granting them economic resources for grass-roots mobilization, that are not as prone to the criticisms of firmer, more institutionalized schemes of "group representation." What she has offered is, in fact, simply a stronger version of equal opportunity—one that might increase the numbers of women and ethnic minorities, as she ably demonstrates by reference to the experience of several European nations. However, she says little if anything about what those representatives *did* while in office. Furthermore, in advancing the case for gender quotas at the party list stage, she ultimately fails to circumvent the essentializing tendencies about which she is rightly concerned. We do not want members of particular groups to have to be the spokespeople for that group and that group alone, but we also want the concerns that are specific to a group or a coalition of groups to be represented, and it seems to me the best way to establish that is to enable groups to organize and speak for themselves.

That seems to warrant the specific empowerment of marginalized groups in the form of economic resources so that the groups themselves can select those members it wants to be included on a slate of candidates. Phillips need not reject groups altogether for consideration of special representation rights. However, she does so because she has premised her analysis upon a commitment to equal treatment as the same treatment (at least with regard to gender—where she argues for a norm of convergence, which is less helpful with regard to race, sexuality, and ethnicity, as she recognizes, but never offers any supplement). Phillips asks, *"What does equality allow?"*

Young forcefully places identity groups in the central location—granting them specific representation and veto rights—which renders her too eager to solidify and institutionalize difference. The cure here might be worse than the disease, however, by facilitating conservatism and diminished deliberation in practice. Although Young is careful to attempt to conceive of the "group" in group representation in non-essentialist ways, the social group veto and the required presence of social group representatives in sub-national level political bodies have the tendency nevertheless to lock in particular understandings of the group (and thus its members), subvert the marginalization of intra-group conflict, and encourage competition rather than cooperation among other groups who could be potential allies.

Guinier has something to offer here with the conception of political race, although as a diagnostic tool political race may not be comprehensive enough to envelop non-race-based systemic biases. Guinier also demonstrates the power and worth of representing interests that need not be so divisive and individualized. "For its part, uncontrolled group representation represents franchise at all costs. The presentation of the demands of oppressed and thus privileged groups in nonnegotiable terms and group perspectives as impenetrable to nonmembers makes authentic democratic interchange impossible and reduces the scope of issues amenable to democratic resolution" (Dryzek 1996, 58). For Young, inclusion is much more central than outcomes, and this emphasis poses particular problems by leaving citizens with little recourse when undesirable or unjust decisions are made.

The concept of a group perspective that Young develops is compelling in many ways. However, it is difficult to imagine what representing perspectives would be like. In addition, if a social group perspective comprises interests, then is not the perspective yet another proxy (and possibly a poor one like race and geography) for interests? Citizens have interests, and insofar as interests are a social concept, they will be shared by groups of citizens. Given that citizen groups are often socially prescribed, this means that those groups are meaningful and they will often share some set of interests that might be called a perspective. However, their interests will conflict at times as well. Furthermore, such focus on rather formal inclusion in representative bodies neglects both the importance of non-state activism and the dangers of absorption and cooptation by an expanded state—or even a global community. John Dryzek points out that "entry into the state can deplete the women's movement of activists who might otherwise push for more radical changes. Something of this sort may have happened in Australia, where women have been more successful in influencing government than they have in most other countries and where 'femocrats' are an established part of government

(Dryzek 1996, 55). Young's scholarship is motivated by the inquiry, *"How can the inclusion of social difference be required?"*

Conclusion: Feminist Theory and Inclusive Representation

While there are multiple and competing forms of democracy, the democratic ideal is an enduring one for its promise of achieving fairness. Yet we can hardly talk about fairness without meaningful inclusion of all citizens and the interests and concerns they bring. What I have attempted to do here is make a case for how historically marginalized groups and the interests they possess, often as a direct result of that very marginalization, might be incorporated in meaningful ways into the public forum. Without such changes, policy will continue to be unreflective of the polity.

More succinctly, what these three feminist scholars provide are the electoral reforms that will provide better opportunities for increased inclusion of historically disadvantaged groups and the interests that are often associated with experiences of marginalization (Guinier), while remaining attuned to the serious potential pitfalls of distinguishing groups in ways that freeze or essentialize differences and mute or ignore intra-group differences (Phillips). Those pitfalls can be avoided (or their effects can be greatly diminished) by understanding the structural nature of difference. The differences that matter are those that structure the lives of groups of citizens that share some characteristic (or set of characteristics) in ways that seriously compromise their life chances or the likelihood of leading a dignified and meaningful life (Young). To this skeletal framework of electoral reform geared toward socially relevant disadvantaged groups, we must add the social obligation to provide the resources by which members of these groups can take advantage of the reformed processes. It is increased participation by members of disadvantaged groups that will ultimately provide the lifeblood that renders procedural reform meaningful by producing fairer outcomes.

At the beginning of this project I proposed that representation for citizens in a democracy requires that (1) all relevant interests be represented in meaningful public policies and practices, and (2) social perspectives or ways of life be recognized and valued. The first criterion has an eye toward particularity while the second is sensitive to the ways in which group affinities structure our lives in meaningful ways that should be recognized rather than assimilated to coincide with a "universal" norm of citizenship. Feminist theory more generally demonstrates the gendered, raced, sexed, and classed determinants of that norm.

Guinier, Phillips, and Young each contribute to a more democratic and fair conception of what representation ought to be, given structures and practices that have created social groups but marginalize them by privileging a citizenship norm they can only attain by denying or subverting important and relevant differences they possess. This representational dilemma will not be solved, however, by asking: *How can electoral reform be meaningful?*; *What does fairness demand?*; or *How can the inclusion of social difference be required?* A more comprehensive and expansive consideration of the law and equality given the reality of social difference is required.

Yet with an emphasis on interests, it is fair to ask to what degree we can expect policy change, must less structural change, that gets at these deeply imbedded problems. That is, even if we adopted everything I have suggested here to facilitate greater inclusion—and it worked at achieving that end—why should we expect more than marginal outcomes? Measures of mass opinion on a variety of key issues related to egalitarianism, such as gay marriage, Affirmative Action, and provisions for social welfare, do not indicate resounding majority support for progressive change. Electoral change for increased inclusion unaccompanied by other key transformations is unlikely to lead to meaningful shifts that affect the kinds of lives that people live.

What we regard as in our interest cannot be but part and parcel of a reflection of the social and historical moment in which we find ourselves. That context, as I have argued here, is acutely and inextricably structured and informed by how we go about organizing and justifying a given distribution of power. Race, class, and gender are human constructions that legitimize unequal and unfair treatment. Indeed one of the greatest legitimizers of inequality is the US system of corporate capitalism. It is not simply an economic system that reinforces social and political stratification, but it is also a cultural force on a par with religion (if it does not in fact supersede it). Key capitalist values such as individualism, competition, and acquisitiveness are indistinguishable from what it means to be an American or even human—and the doctrine of American Exceptionalism both conflates these two concepts and simultaneously elevates US superiority and distinctiveness. The result is a cultural context that rewards behavior that aligns with capitalist values. The ever-present and unrelenting force of this cultural narrative that masquerades as reality makes it very difficult to identify and resist. Instead, most citizens develop a set of interests that align with, or at least are not hostile to, the capitalist order. Meaningful political representation must also include measures to intervene in this hegemony such that notions about meaningful equality can gain some kind of footing.

Fair representation thus means that historically marginalized groups should be granted the resources to organize and develop slates of candidates that share their interests, and those candidates should be elected from broad jurisdictions that operate under a system of representation that employs cumulative voting. Experiments to achieve a greater presence of members of historically marginalized groups show real promise for increasing the representation of their interests, for example, in India on local councils, in Scandinavian countries on national legislatures, and even in the United States, where experiments at local and state levels as well as within the national party structures have produced policies and expanded agendas, and altered the very terms of debates that probably would have otherwise remained unchanged. How to go about increasing this presence, however, is a highly complex endeavor fraught with potential, but very real, dangers. Yet movements like the one in South Carolina to remove the Confederate flag from atop the statehouse dome are examples of public philosophy, or moral and ethical considerations, put into political action (Sandel 2005). Coalitions are possible, especially when movement participants are empowered to inform the language, conditions, and context of public debate—and coalitions, as Laura Woliver's study of four citizen groups illustrates, are "stronger than groups made up of mobilized individuals alone" since coalitions are less likely to be ignored as representatives of irrelevant and specialized interests by those in power, and the members of those coalitions are thereby less prone to become disillusioned and defect (Woliver 1993, 153). Moreover it is in group settings, as Doug McAdam reminds us, that injustice can even be named. So long as we remain separate and silent, oppression is simply a series of incidents that can be explained by bad luck, accident, or, even more often, "just the way things are." "[S]egments of society may very well submit to oppressive conditions unless that oppression is collectively defined as both unjust and *subject to change*" (McAdam 1982, 34; emphasis in the original). The solution is along the razor's edge. An emphasis on interests respects the cross-cutting nature of identity or social position while the careful recognition of groups refuses to ignore their significance or freeze their meaning.

Bibliography

Ackerman, Bruce, 1984. *Reconstructing American Law*. Cambridge, MA: Harvard University Press.

Amy, Douglas J., 1993. *Real Choices/New Voices: The Case for Proportional Representation in the United States*. New York: Columbia University Press.

Andersen, Kristi, 1996. *After Suffrage: Women in Partisan and Electoral Politics before the New Deal*. Chicago, IL: The University of Chicago Press.

APSA Task Force on Inequality and American Democracy, 2004. American Democracy in an age of rising inequality. *Perspectives on Politics* 2 (4): 651–66.

Armstrong, Chris, 2000. Which inequalities matter? *Political Quarterly* 71 (3): 367–8.

Bachrach, Peter and Morton S. Baratz, 1962. The two faces of power. *American Political Science Review* 56 (4): 947–52.

Baer, Judith A., 1999. *Our Lives Before the Law: Constructing a Feminist Jurisprudence*. Princeton, NJ: Princeton University Press.

Barber, Benjamin, 1984. *Strong Democracy: Participatory Politics for a New Age*. Berkeley, CA: University of California Press.

Barber, Kathleen L., 2000. *A Right to Representation: Proportional Election Systems for the Twenty-first Century*. Columbus, OH: Ohio State University Press.

Barry, Brian, 2001. *Culture and Equality: An Egalitarian Critique of Multiculturalism*. Cambridge, MA: Harvard University Press.

Bell, Derrick A., Jr, 1995. Serving two masters: integration ideals and client interests in school desegregation litigation, in Kimberlé Crenshaw, et al., eds, *Critical Race Theory*. New York: The New Press.

Bell, Derrick A., Jr, 2000. *Race, Racism, and American Law*. New York: Aspen.

Benhabib, Seyla, 1992. *Situating the Self: Gender, Community and Postmodernism in Contemporary Ethics*. New York: Routledge, Chapman & Hall.

Benhabib, Seyla, ed., 1996. *Democracy and Difference: Contesting the Boundaries of the Political*. Princeton, NJ: Princeton University Press.

Benhabib, Seyla, 2002. *The Claims of Culture: Equality and Diversity in the Global Era*. Princeton, NJ: Princeton University Press.

Bennett, Stephen Earl and David Resnick, 1990. Implications of nonvoting for democracy and the United States. *American Journal of Political Science* 34: 771–803.

Berry, Jeffrey M., Kent E. Portney, and Ken Thomson, 1993. *The Rebirth of Urban Democracy*. Washington, DC: The Brookings Institution.

Bérubé, Michael, 2003. Testing Handicaps. *The New York Times Magazine*, September 21: 18.

Bickford, Susan, 1999. Reconfiguring pluralism: identity and institutions in the inegalitarian polity. *American Political Science Review* 33 (1): 86–108.

Black, Earl and Merle Black, 2002. *The Rise of Southern Republicans*. Cambridge, MA: The Belknap Press of Harvard University Press.

Bladuell, Hèctor G., 2001/2002. Race and social justice movements: Lanie Guinier and Gerald Torres, *The Miner's Canary: Enlisting Race, Resisting Power, Transforming Democracy*. *Harvard Journal of Hispanic Policy* 14: 135–40.

Blais, Andre and A. Dobrzynska, 1998. Turnout in electoral democracies. *European Journal of Political Research* 33 (2): 239–61.

Blau, Francine D. and Lawrence M. Kahn, 1994. Rising wage inequality and the U.S. gender gap. *The American Economic Review* 84 (2): 23–8.

Bourdieu, Pierre, 1990. *The Logic of Practice*. Stanford, CA: Stanford University Press.

Bowler, Shaun, Todd Donovan, and David Brockington, 2003. *Electoral Reform and Minority Representation: Local Experiments with Alternative Elections*. Columbus, OH: The Ohio State University Press.

Bronner, Stephen Eric, 1999. *Ideas in Action: Political Tradition in the Twentieth Century*. Lanham, MD: Rowman & Littlefield.

Brooks, David, 2006. Bye-bye, Bootstraps. *The New York Times*, August 3: A21.

Brown, Wendy, 1995. *States of Injury: Power and Freedom in Late Modernity*. Princeton, NJ: Princeton University Press.

Burns, Nancy, Kay Lehman Schlozman, and Sidney Verba, 1997. The public consequences of private inequality: family life and citizen participation. *American Political Science Review* 91 (2): 373–89.

Burns, Nancy, Kay Lehman Schlozman, and Sidney Verba, 2001. *The Private Roots of Public Action: Gender, Equality, and Political Participation*. Cambridge, MA: Harvard University Press.

Burrell, Barbara, 1994. *A Woman's Place is in the House: Campaigning for Congress in the Feminist Era*. Ann Arbor, MI: University of Michigan Press.

Butler, Judith, 1990. *Gender Trouble: Feminism and the Subversion of Identity*. New York: Routledge.

Butler, Judith, 1997. *Excitable Speech: A Politics of the Performative*. New York: Routledge.

Butler, Judith and Joan Scott, eds, 1992. *Feminists Theorize the Political.* New York: Routledge.

Chong, Dennis, 1991. *Collective Action and the Civil Rights Movement*. Chicago, IL: University of Chicago Press.

Christiano, Thomas, 1990. Freedom, consensus, and equality in collective decisionmaking. *Ethics* 101 (1): 151–81.

Christiano, Thomas, 1996. *The Rule of the Many*. Boulder, CO: Westview Press.

Chwe, Michael Suk-Young, 1999. Minority voting rights can maximize majority welfare. *American Political Science Review* 93 (1): 85–97.

Civil Rights Project at Harvard University, 2002. www.law.harvard.edu/civilrights/publications/reseg_districts02/Race_in_American_Public_Schools1.pdf.

Cohen, Cathy J., 1997. Straight gay politics: the limits of an ethnic model of inclusion, in Ian Shapiro and Will Kymlicka, eds, *Nomos XXXIX: Ethnicity and Group Rights*. New York: New York University Press.

Collins, Patricia Hill, 2000. *Black Feminist Thought: Knowledge, Consciousness, and the Politics of Empowerment*. New York: Routledge.

Cornell, Drucilla, 1992. *Deconstruction and the Possibility of Justice*. New York: Routledge, Chapman and Hall.

Cornell, Drucilla, 1999. *Beyond Accommodation: Ethical Feminism, Deconstruction, and the Law*. New York: Roman & Littlefield.

Cornell, Drucilla, 2000. *Just Cause: Freedom, Identity, and Rights*. New York: Roman & Littlefield.

Costain, Anne N., 1992. *Inviting Women's Rebellion.* Baltimore, MD: The Johns Hopkins University.

Crenshaw, Kimberlé, 1995. Race, reform, and retrenchment: transformation and legitimation in anti-discrimination law, in Kimberlé Crenshaw, et al., eds, *Critical Race Theory*. New York: The New Press.

Crenshaw, Kimberlé, 1998. Demarginalizing the intersection of race and sex: a black feminist critique of antidiscrimination doctrine, feminist theory and antiracist politics. *Chicago Legal Forum*: 139–67.

Crigler, Ann N., Marion R. Just, and Edward J. McCaffery, 2004. *Rethinking the Vote: The Politics and Prospects of American Election Reform*. New York: Oxford University Press.

Cruikshank, Barbara, 2002. *Review of Democracy and Inclusion* in the *American Political Science Review* 96 (1): 200–1.

Dahl, Robert, 1963. *Who Governs?* New Haven, CT: Yale University Press.

Dahl, Robert, 1972. *Polyarchy.* New Haven, CT: Yale University Press.

Dahl, Robert, 1989. *Democracy and Its Critics.* New Haven, CT: Yale University Press.

Dahl, Robert, 2003. *How Democratic is the American Constitution?* New Haven, CT: Yale University Press.

Dahl, Robert and Charles Lindblom, 1983. Comment on Manley. *American Political Science Review* 77 (2): 384–9.

Dalton, Harlon L., 1995. The clouded prism: minority critique of the critical legal studies movement, in Kimberlé Crenshaw, et al., eds, *Critical Race Theory*. New York: The New Press.

de la Garza, Rodolfo O., 1995. The effects of ethnicity on political culture, in Paul E. Peterson, ed., *Classifying by Race*. Princeton, NJ: Princeton University Press.

Disch, Lisa J., 2002. *The Tyranny of the Two-party System*. New York: Columbia University Press.

Dovi, Suzanne, 2002. Preferable descriptive representatives: will just any woman, black, Latino do? *American Political Science Review* 96 (4): 729–43.

Dryzek, John, 1996. *Democracy in Capitalist Times: Ideals, Limits, and Struggles*. New York: Oxford University Press.

Dworkin, Ronald, 1977. *Taking Rights Seriously.* Cambridge, MA: Harvard University Press.

Dworkin, Ronald, 2000. *Sovereign Virtue*. Cambridge, MA: Harvard University Press.

Edelman, Murray, 1988. *Constructing the Political Spectacle*. Chicago, IL: The University of Chicago Press.

Eldersveld, Samuel J., and Hanes Walton, Jr, 2000. *Political Parties in American Society*. New York: Bedford/St Martin's.

Ellis, Richard J., 1993. *American Political Cultures*. New York: Oxford University Press.

Engstrom, Richard L., and Charles J. Barrilleaux. 1991. Native Americans and cumulative voting: the Sisseton Wahpeton Sioux. *Social Science Quarterly* 72: 388–93.

Engstrom, Richard L., Delbert A. Taebel, and Richard L. Cole. 1989. Cumulative voting as a remedy for minority vote dilution: the case of Alamogordo, New Mexico. *Journal of Law and Politics* 5: 469–97.

Engstrom, Richard L., Jason F. Kirksey, and Edward Still. 1997. Limited and cumulative voting in Alabama: an assessment after two rounds of elections. *National Political Science Review* 6: 180–91.

Fineman, Martha, 1991. *The Illusion of Equality: The Rhetoric and Reality of Divorce Reform*. Chicago, IL: University of Chicago Press.

Fixing Democracy, 2004. *The New York Times*, January 18: 10.

Flammang, Janet, 1997. *Women's Political Voice: How Women are Transforming the Practice and Study of Politics*. Philadelphia, PA: Temple University Press.

Fogg-Davis, Hawley, 2003. The racial retreat of contemporary political theory. *Perspectives on Politics* 1 (3): 555–64.

Foucault, Michel, 1990. *The History of Sexuality, Volume I: An Introduction*. New York: Vintage Books.

Frankenberg, Erica Chumgmei Lee, and Gary Orfield, 2002. *A Multiracial Society with Segregated Schools: Are We Losing the Dream?* Cambridge, MA: Harvard Civil Rights Project.

Fraser, Nancy, Axel Honneth, and Christiane Wilke, 2003. *Redistribution or Recognition?: A Political–Philosophical Exchange*. New York: Verso Books.

Gaventa, John, 1982. *Power and Powerlessness: Quiescence and Rebellion in an Appalachian Valley*. Chicago, IL: University of Illinois Press.

Graber, Mark A., 1996. Conflicting representations: Lani Guinier and James Madison on electoral systems. *Constitutional Commentary* 13 (3): 291–308.

Guinier, Lani, 1994. *The Tyranny of the Majority*. New York: The Free Press.

Guinier, Lani, 1995. Groups, representation, and race-conscious districting: a case of the emperor's clothes, in Kimberlé Crenshaw, et al., eds, *Critical Race Theory*. New York: The New Press.

Guinier, Lani and Gerald Torres, 2002. *The Miner's Canary: Enlisting Race, Resisting Power, Transforming Democracy*. Cambridge, MA: Harvard University Press.

Gurr, Ted R., 1971. *Why Men Rebel*. Princeton, NJ: Princeton University Press.

Gutman, Amy, ed., 1992. *Multiculturalism and the "Politics of Recognition"*. Princeton, NJ: Princeton University Press.

Gutman, Amy, 1993. The challenge of multiculturalism to political ethics. *Philosophy and Public Affairs* 22 (3): 171–206.

Gutmann, Amy and Dennis Thompson, 1996. *Democracy and Disagreement*. Cambridge, MA: Belknap Press of Harvard University Press.

Habermas, Jürgen, 1985. *The Theory of Communicative Action*. Boston, MA: Beacon Press.

Harris, Cheryl I., 1995. Whiteness as property, in Kimberlé Crenshaw, et al., eds, *Critical Race Theory*. New York: The New Press.

Hartsock, Nancy, 1999. *The Feminist Standpoint Revisited and Other Essays*. Boulder, CO: Westview Press.

Hero, Rodney E. and Caroline J. Tolbert. 1995. Latinos and substantive representation in the U.S. House of Representatives: direct, indirect, or nonexistent? *American Journal of Political Science* 39 (3): 640–52.

Hirschmann, Nancy J. and Christine Di Stefano, 1996. *Revisioning the Political: Feminist Reconstructions of Traditional Concepts in Western Political Theory*. Boulder, CO: Westview Press.

Hodgkiss, Anita. 1999. Prepared Statement Concerning H.R. 1173, States' Choice of Voting Systems Act, before the Subcommittee on the Constitution, Committee on the Judiciary, US House of Representatives, Washington, DC, September 23.

hooks, bell, 1990. *Yearning: Race, Gender, and Cultural Politics.* Boston, MA: South End Press.

hooks, bell, 1992. *Black Looks: Race and Representation*. Boston, MA: South End Press.

hooks, bell, 2000. *Feminist Theory From Margin to Center*. Boston, MA: South End Press.

Htun, Mala, 2004. Is Gender Like Ethnicity? The Political Representation of Identity Groups. *Perspectives on Politics* 2 (3), 439–58.

Jackman, Robert W., 1987. Political insitutions and voter turnout in the industrialized democracies. *American Political Science Review* 81 (2): 405–24.

Jackman, Robert W. and Ross A. Miller, 1995. Voter turnout in industrialized democracies during the 1980s. *Comparative Political Studies* 27: 467–92.

Jaggar, Alison M., 1983. *Feminist Politics and Human Nature*. New York: Roman & Littlefield.

James, Michael Rabinder, 2004. *Deliberative Democracy and the Plural Polity*. Lawrence, KS: University Press of Kansas.

Jeon, Deborah, 1999. Cumulative voting imposed in Maryland County. http://www.fairvote.org/reports/1995/chp5/jeon.html.

King, Richard H., 1997. The Politics of Presence. *Ethnic and Racial Studies* 20 (4): 850–2.

Kirn, Walter, 2006. Way Upstairs, Downstairs, *The New York Times Magazine*, April 16, 2006.

Kukathas, Chandran, 1997. Cultural Toleration, in Ian Shapiro and Will Kymlicka, eds, *Nomos XXXIX: Ethnicity and Group Rights*. New York: New York University Press.

Kymlicka, Will, 1995. *Multicultural Citizenship*. New York: Oxford University Press.

Ladner, A. and H. Milner, 1999. Do voters turn out more under proportional than majoritarian systems? The evidence from Swiss communal elections. *Electoral Studies* 18 (2): 235–50.

Lijphart, Arend, 1984. *Patterns of Majoritarian and Consensus Government in Twenty-one Countries*. New Haven, CT: Yale University Press.

Lijphart, Arend, 1999. *Patterns of Democracy: Government Forms and Performance in Thirty-six Countries*. New Haven, CT: Yale University Press.

Lublin, David, 1999. *The Paradox of Representation*. Princeton, NJ: Princeton University Press.

Luker, Kristin, 1984. *Abortion and the Politics of Motherhood*. Los Angeles, CA: University of California Press.

Lukes, Stephen, 2004. *Power: A Radical View*. New York: Palgrave Macmillan.

Macedo, Stephen, ed., 2005. *Democracy at Risk: How Political Choices Undermine Citizen Participation and What We Can Do About It*. Washington, DC: The Brookings Insitution.

MacKinnon, Catherine A., 1989. *Toward a Feminist Theory of the State*. Cambridge, MA: Harvard University Press.

Manley, John F., 1983. Neo-pluralism: a class analysis of pluralism I and pluralism II. *The American Political Science Review* 77 (2): 368–83.

Mansbridge, Jane, 1983. *Beyond Adversary Democracy*. Chicago, IL: University of Chicago Press.

Mansbridge, Jane, 2003. Rethinking representation. *American Political Science Review* 97 (4): 515–28.

Manza, Jeff, and Christopher Uggen, 2004. Punishment and democracy: disenfranchisement of non-incarcerated felons in the United States. *Perspectives on Politics* 2 (3): 491–505.

Matsuda, Mari, 1995. Looking to the bottom: Critical Legal Studies and Reparations, in Kimberlé Crenshaw, et al., eds, *Critical Race Theory*. New York: The New Press.

Matsuda, Mari, and Charles R. Lawrence, III, 1993. *Words That Wound: Critical Race Theory, Assaultive Speech, and the First Amendment*. Boulder, CO: Westview Press.

McAdam, Doug, 1982. *Political Process and the Development of Black Insurgency, 1930– 1970*. Chicago, IL: The University of Chicago Press.

Minow, Martha, 1990. *Making All the Difference*. Ithaca, NY: Cornell University Press.

Minow, Martha, 1991. From class action to Miss Saigon: the concept of representation in the law. *Cleveland State Law Review* 39: 269–300.

Minow, Martha, 1993. The Supreme Court 1986 Term, Foreword: Justice Engendered, in D. Kelly Weisberg ed., *Feminist Legal Theory: Foundations*. Philadelphia: Temple University Press.

Minow, Martha, 1997. *Not Only for Myself: Identity, Politics, and the Law*. New York: The New Press.

Morrison, Toni, 1997. Disturbing nurses and the kindness of sharks, in Catherine Belsey and Jane Moore, eds, *The Feminist Reader*. Malden, MA: Blackwell.

Mulroy, Steven, 1995. Limited, cumulative evidence: divining justice department positions on alternative electoral systems. *National Civic Review* 84: 66–71.

Murrell, Audrey J. and Ray Jones, 1996. Assessing affirmative action: past, present, and future. *Journal of Social Issues* 52 (4): 77–92.

Nussbaum, Martha C., 1999. *Sex and Social Justice*. New York: Oxford University Press.

Office of Management and Budget , 2010. Budget of the U.S. Government FY 2011, historical Tables, Table 2.2, http://www.gpoaccess.gov//usbudget/fy11/sheets/hist02z2.xls (accessed May 3, 2010).

Okin, Susan Moller, 1999. *Is Multiculturalism Bad for Women?* Princeton, NJ: Princeton University Press.

Olson, Mancur, 1965. *The Logic of Collective Action*. Cambridge, MA: Harvard University Press.

On the Money Trail, 2004. *The Atlantic Monthly* 293 (3): 48.

Pateman, Carole, 1970. *Participation and Democratic Theory*. Cambridge: Cambridge University Press.

Pateman, Carole, 1988. *The Sexual Contract*. Stanford, CA: Stanford University Press.

Pateman, Carole, 1989. *The Disorder of Women: Democracy, Feminism and Political Theory*. Stanford, CA: Stanford University Press.

Phelan, Shane, 1989. *Identity Politics*. Philadelphia, PA: Temple University Press.

Phelan, Shane, 1994. *Getting Specific: Postmodern Lesbian Politics*. Minneapolis, MN: University of Minnesota Press.

Phillips, Anne, 1991. *Engendering Democracy*. University Park, PA: The Pennsylvania State University Press.

Phillips, Anne, 1993. *Democracy and Difference*. University Park, PA: The Pennsylvania State University Press.

Phillips, Anne, 1995. *The Politics of Presence: Issues in Democracy and Group Representation*. New York: Oxford University Press.

Phillips, Anne, 1998. *Feminism and Politics*. Oxford: Oxford University Press.

Phillips, Anne, 1999. *Which Inequalities Matter*. Malden, MA: Polity Press.

Pitkin, Hanna Fenichel, 1967. *The Concept of Representation*. Los Angeles, CA: The University of California Press.

Piven, Frances Fox, 2006. *Challenging Authority: How Ordinary People Change America*. New York: Roman & Littlefield.

Piven, Frances Fox, and Richard A. Cloward, 1979. *Poor People's Movements: Why They Succeed, How They Fail*. New York: Pantheon Books.

Powell, G. Bingham, 1986. American voter turnout in comparative perspective. *American Political Science Review* 80 (1): 17–43.

Rawls, John, 1971. A *Theory of Justice.* Cambridge, MA: Harvard University Press.

Rawls, John, 1993. *Political Liberalism.* New York: Columbia University Press.

Raz, Joseph, 1983. *The Authority of Law: Essays on Law and Morality.* Oxford: Clarendon Press.

Raz, Joseph, 1994. *Ethics in the Public Domain: Essays in the Morality of Law and Politics.* New York: Oxford University Press.

Rhode, Deborah L., 1989. *Justice and Gender.* Cambridge, MA: Harvard University Press.

Roberts, Dorothy E., 1998. *Killing the Black Body: Race, Reproduction, and the Meaning of Liberty.* New York: Vintage.

Rosenberg, Gerald N., 1993. *The Hollow Hope: Can Courts Bring About Social Change?* Chicago, IL: University of Chicago Press.

Rule, Wilma, and Joseph F. Zimmerman, 1992. *United States Electoral Systems: Their Impact on Women and Minorities.* New York: Greenwood Press.

Rule, Wilma and Joseph F. Zimmerman, 1994. *Electoral Systems in Comparative Perspective: Their Impact on Women and Minorities.* Westport, CT: Greenwood Press.

Rush, Mark E. and Richard L. Engstrom, 2001. *Fair and Effective Representation?* New York: Roman & Littlefield.

Sandel. Michael J., 2005. *Public Philosophy: Essays on Morality in Politics.* Cambridge, MA: Harvard University Press.

Scott, James, 1985. *Weapons of the Weak: Everyday Forms of Peasant Resistance.* New Haven, CT: Yale University Press.

Scott, James, 1990. *Domination and the Arts of Resistance: Hidden Transcripts.* New Haven, CT: Yale University Press.

Semple, Kirk, 2010. Trying to make history, with six votes per person. *The New York Times*, June 12: A14 and A27.

Singer, Mark, 2002. A Year of Trouble. *The New Yorker*, May 20: 42–6.

Spitz, Elaine, 1984. *Majority Rule.* Chatham, NJ: Chatham House.

Squires, Judith, 2000. Group representation, deliberation and the displacement of dichotomies, in Michael Saward, ed., *Democratic Innovation: Deliberation, Representation and Association.* New York: Routledge.

Steinberg, Jacques, 2002. Using synonyms for race, college strives for diversity. *New York Times*, December 8: 22 and 45.

Stone, Deborah, 2002. *Policy Paradox: The Art of Political Decision Making.* New York: W.W. Norton.

Sullivan, Andrew, 1996. *Virtually Normal: An Argument About Homosexuality.* New York: Vintage.

Sunstein, Cass R., 1994. *The Partial Constitution*. Cambridge, MA: Harvard University Press.

Tarrow, Sidney, 1998. *Power in Movement*. New York: Cambridge University Press.

Tebble, Adam James, 2002. What is the politics of difference? *Political Theory* 30 (2): 259–81.

The Thick Red Line, 2004. *The Atlantic Monthly*, April: 44. Full ACORN report can be accessed at http://www.acorn.org/fileadmin/Community_Reinvestment/Reports/Great_Divide_2003_Main.pdf.

Thomas, Sue, 1994. *How Women Legislate*. New York: Oxford University Press.

Tilly, Charles, 1984. Social movements and national politics, in C. Bright and S. Harding, eds, *Statemaking and Social Movements: Essays in History and Theory*. Ann Arbor, MI: University of Michigan Press, 297–317.

Tilly, Charles, 1990. *Coercion, Capital, and European States, 990–1990*. Cambridge, MA: Blackwell.

Tilly, Charles, 2001. Which inequalities matter? *Theory, Culture, and Society* 18 (4): 129–33.

Tilly, Charles, 2003. *The Politics of Collective Violence*. New York: Cambridge University Press.

Tocqueville, Alexis, 1969. *Democracy in America*. New York: Harper Perennial.

Toobin, Jeffrey, 2003. The great election grab. *The New Yorker*, December 8: 63–80.

US Department of Justice Prison Statistics, 2004. http://www.ojp.usdoj.gov/bjs/prisons.htm.

Verba, Sidney, Kay Lehman Schlozman, and Henry Brady, 1995. Race, ethnicity, and political participation, in Paul E. Peterson, ed., *Classifying by Race*. Princeton, NJ: Princeton University Press

Verba, Sidney, Kay Lehman Schlozman, Henry Brady, and Norman H. Nie, 1993. Citizen activity: who participates? What do they say? *American Political Science Review* 87 (2): 303–18.

Verba, Sidney, Nancy Burns, and Kay Lehman Schlozman, 1997. Knowing and caring about politics: gender and political engagement. *Journal of Politics* 59 (4): 1051–72.

Walzer, Michael, 1983. *Spheres of Justice: A Defense of Pluralism and Equality*. New York: Basic Books.

Warren, Mark E., 2002. Iris Marion Young, *Inclusion and Democracy*. [Review.] *Ethics* 112: 646–50.

Weber, Lynn, 2001. *Understanding Race, Class, Gender and Sexuality: A Conceptual Framework*. Boston, MA: McGraw-Hill.

Williams, Melissa, 1998. *Voice, Trust, and Memory*. Princeton, NJ: Princeton University Press.

Williams, Patricia J., 1992. *The Alchemy of Race and Rights*. Cambridge, MA: Harvard University Press.

Wolin, Sheldon, 2010. *Democracy Incorporated: Managed Democracy and the Specter of Inverted Totalitarianism*. Princeton, NJ: Princeton University Press.

Woliver, Laura R., 1993. *From Outrage to Action: The Politics of Grass-roots Dissent*. Chicago, IL: University of Illinois Press.

Woliver, Laura R., Angela D. Ledford, and Chris J. Dolan, 2001. The South Carolina Confederate flag: the politics of race and citizenship. *Politics and Policy*, 29 (4), 708–30.

Women in National Parliaments, 2003. http://www.ipu.org/wmn-e/classif.htm

Yang, Alan S., 1997. Attitudes toward homosexuality. *Public Opinion Quarterly* 61, 477–507.

Young, Iris Marion, 1990. *Justice and the Politics of Difference*. Princeton, NJ: Princeton University Press.

Young, Iris Marion, 1993. Together in difference: transforming the logic of group political conflict, in Judith Squires, ed., *Principled Positions: Postmodernism and the Rediscovery of Value*. London: Lawrence and Wishart, 121–50.

Young, Iris Marion, 1997. *Intersecting Voices: Dilemmas of Gender, Political Philosophy, and Policy*. Princeton, NJ: Princeton University Press.

Young, Iris Marion, 2000. *Inclusion and Democracy*. New York: Oxford University Press.

Zimmerman, Joseph F. and Wilma Rule, 2000. *The U.S. House of Representatives: Reform or Rebuild?* Westport, CT: Praeger.

Zweig, Michael, 2004. *What's Class Got to Do With It? American Society in the Twentieth Century*. Ithaca: Cornell University Press.

Index

abortion 15–16
accountability 48–9
Affirmative Action 36–7, 38, 39–40
African-Americans 98
agency 119, 122
Agency for a Strong Democracy 99, 100, 101
alternative voting systems 89–97
Amy, D.J. 90
Andersen, K. 53, 106
anti-flag coalition (Confederate flag) 27–8, 137
APSA Taskforce Report on Inequality and American Democracy 53–4
Armstrong, C. 60–61

Barber, B. 96
Barry, B. 74, 82–3, 87
Berry, J.M. et al. 100, 101
Bérubé, M. 4
Bladuell, H.G. 42
boundary activation 98–9
Bourdieu, P. 47, 114
Bronner, S.E. 112
Brooks, D. 126
Burns, N. et al. 124–5

candidate-centred elections 95
Christiano, T. 93, 96, 103, 104, 122, 125
Chwe, M.S.-Y. 28–9
citizenship 7, 135
    citizen/worker and resistance 119–22
    rational citizen, concept of 81–2
class *see* social class
coalition politics, political race and 31–3
Cohen, C.J. 41
collective violence 98–9
community action program (CAP) 99–101, 106–7
Confederate flag (anti-flag coalition) 27–8, 137
Crenshaw, K. 35, 38–9, 129
Crigler, A.N. et al. 122–3
Cruikshank, B. 81
cultural groups 87
cumulative voting 26, 89–91, 92–3, 96, 125, 131

Dahl, R. 97, 102–3, 107, 119–20
deliberative democracy 77–82, 84, 85, 103
democratic dialogue 69
descriptive representatives 104–5
difference
    and deliberative democracy 77–82, 84, 85, 103
    "equality through difference" 8
    "freezing differences" 51–2, 59
    representation of 67–76, 82–7
Disch, L.J. 94
districting 24, 25–7, 131, 132
Dovi, S. 61, 73, 104–5
Droop quota 92
Dryzek, J. 134–5

education
    higher, race and 2–4, 39–40
    transforming social processes 118–19
electoral system and reform 24–31, 89–97, 135
"equality through difference" 8

fair representation 135–7
    political parties and 52–9
feminist intersectional standpoint 12–13
feminist theory 6–8, 129–31, 135–7
Fogg-Davis, H. 32–3
Foucault, M. 67
"freezing differences" 51–2, 59
funding 58, 86, 99–104

fusion, concept of 94

gay/lesbian issues 7, 41–2
gender convergence 51–2
gender quotas 50, 55–6, 57, 62, 63, 64, 65, 105–6, 133
Graber, M.A. 29, 30, 31
greetings in deliberative democracy 79
group perspective 72, 134–5
    interests and perspectives 14–19, 72–3
group representation, critique of 48–51, 63–6
Guinier, L. 8–10, 12, 18, 21–45, 130, 131–3, 134, 135, 136

habitus 114
higher education 2–4, 39–40
hooks, b. 89
Htun, M. 54–6

inclusion norm 86
inclusive citizenship 7
inclusive representation 12–13, 135–7
inequalities, political and social 1–6
"instant run-off voting" 91
interests
    groups and 14–19, 72–3
    manufactured, and resistance 115–17

Jaggar, A.M. 6
Jeon, D. 90–91

Kirn, W. 126

legal subjectivity 22–4
lesbian/gay issues 7, 41–2
limited voting 89–90, 91, 93, 96
Luker, K. 15–16

McAdam, D. 41, 43, 127, 137
McKinney, C. 47
majority rule 76, 83, 107
    supermajorities and 75–6
Mansbridge, J. 14–15, 25
Minow, M. 22–3
Morrison, T. 21
multi-party and two-party systems 94–5
multiculturalism 74, 82, 87

Native Americans 56, 71, 73–4, 75

Olsen, M. 16–17

participatory democracy 76, 77
party list quotas 49, 53, 57–8
    gender 50, 55–6, 57, 62, 63, 64, 65, 105–6, 133
    and slates of electors 59
Phelan, S. 7, 65–6
Phillips, A. 10–11, 12, 18–19, 47–66, 130, 133, 135, 136
Pitkin, H. 13, 29, 30, 48–9
Piven, F.F. 118–19
    and Cloward, R.A. 118–19
political development scholarship 17–18
political identity, political race and 33–44
political participation 122–7
political parties
    electoral change and 89–97
    and fair representation 52–9
political race 31–44, 132–3, 134
political and social inequalities 1–6
power and social class 112–15, 116
preference voting 91–2, 93
proportional representation (PR) 71–2
    semi- 93, 95–6
    see also party list quotas
public funding 58, 86, 99–104

race
    African-Americans 98
    higher education 2–4, 39–40
    Native Americans 56, 71, 73–4, 75
    political 31–44, 132–3, 134
    political and social inequalities 1–6
race-conscious districting 24, 26–7, 132
racial bribe 42
rational citizen, concept of 81–2
recognition and redistribution 60–63
resistance *see under* social class
rhetoric in deliberative democracy 79–80
Rhode, D.L. 22
Rice University 2
Rush, M.E. and Engstrom, R.L. 89–90, 91, 92, 93, 96–7

Scott, J. 118–19

Singer, M. 41–2
situated knowledge in deliberative democracy 80
slates of electors 59
  Electoral College 94–5
social class 42, 102–3, 109–11
  political participation 122–7
  political representation 111–12, 122–5
  and power 112–15, 116
  resistance
    citizen/worker and 119–22
    manufactured interests and 115–17
  transforming social processes: education 118–19
social and political inequalities 1–6
Spitz, E. 1
Steinberg, J. 2
Stone, D. 13, 106–7
structured groups
  characteristics 69
  and cultural groups 70
  inclusion norm 86
  and social perspective 70–71, 84–6
supermajorities 75–6
surrogate representation 25

"The Thick Red Line" 98
Tilly, C. 43, 98–9
Toqueville, A. de 21
Torres, G. 23, 31–2, 33–6, 38, 39–40, 42–3, 44, 132–3
two-party and multi-party systems 94–5

under-representation 4–5

Verba, S. et al. 123–4
veto rights 73–5, 85, 134
violence, collective 98–9
virtual representation 25
votes/voting
  alternative systems 89–97
  cumulative 26, 89–91, 92–3, 96, 125, 131
  Electoral College 94–5
  "instant run-off voting" 91
  limited 89–90, 91, 93, 96
  preference 91–2, 93
  wasted 24–5, 94
  women 106

Warren, M.E. 84
wasted votes 24–5, 94
Weber, L. 37, 129
Williams, M. 92
Woliver, L.R. et al. 28, 137
women
  abortion 15–16
  pluralization of representation 102
  voting right 106
working class 113–14
  see also social class

Young, I.M. 11–12, 19, 56, 58, 67–87, 98, 130, 132, 134–5, 136

Zweig, M. 113–14

www.ingramcontent.com/pod-product-compliance
Ingram Content Group UK Ltd.
Pitfield, Milton Keynes, MK11 3LW, UK
UKHW011018180926
475701UK00004B/810
* 9 7 8 1 1 3 8 2 7 8 8 1 3 *